Building Blocks of Religion

BUILDING BLOCKS OF RELIGION

Critical Applications and Future Prospects

Edited by Göran Larsson, Jonas Svensson,
and Andreas Nordin

SHEFFIELD UK   BRISTOL CT

Published by Equinox Publishing Ltd.

UK: Office 415, The Workstation, 15 Paternoster Row, Sheffield S1 2BX
USA: ISD, 70 Enterprise Drive, Bristol, CT 06010

www.equinoxpub.com

First published 2020

© Göran Larsson, Jonas Svensson, Andreas Nordin and contributors 2020

All rights reserved. No part of this publication may be reproduced or transmitted in any form or by any means, electronic or mechanical, including photocopying, recording or any information storage or retrieval system, without prior permission in writing from the publishers.

ISBN 978 1 78179 866 9   (hardback)
      978 1 78179 867 6   (paperback)
      978 1 78179 868 3   (ePDF)

British Library Cataloguing-in-Publication Data

A catalogue record for this book is available from the British Library.

Library of Congress Cataloging-in-Publication Data

Names: Larsson, Göran, editor.
Title: Building blocks of religion : critical applications and future prospects / edited by Göran Larsson, Jonas Svensson, and Andreas Nordin.
Description: Bristol : Equinox Publishing Ltd., 2020. | Includes bibliographical references and index.
Identifiers: LCCN 2019013633 (print) | ISBN 9781781798669 (hb) | ISBN 9781781798676 (pb)
Subjects: LCSH: Religion.
Classification: LCC BL25 .B85 2020 (print) | LCC BL25 (ebook) | DDC 200--dc23
LC record available at https://lccn.loc.gov/2019013633
LC ebook record available at https://lccn.loc.gov/2019980254

Typeset by CA Typesetting Ltd, Sheffield, UK

Contents

Preface
Göran Larsson, Andreas Nordin, and Jonas Svensson   vii

By Way of Introduction
Göran Larsson, Andreas Nordin, and Jonas Svensson   1

1   The Building Block Approach: An Overview
     Ann Taves and Egil Asprem   5

2   Between a Rock and a Hard Place:
     Analysing the Reception of and Debate
     over the Building Block Approach
     Göran Larsson   26

3   Fantastic Stories, Emotions, and Ancient Religions:
     Open Questions and Ideas in Conversation with the
     Building Block and Worldviews Approach
     Laura Feldt   39

4   Counterintuitive Supernaturalism as a Building Block
     of Religious Dream Imagery
     Andreas Nordin   55

5   Invisible Hands and Sacred Unicorns:
     Occulture as a Schema for Supernatural
     Ascriptions in the Millennial Generation
     Ingela Visuri   71

6   Qur'ans through the Lens of Moral Foundations:
     An Explorative Study of Qur'an Translations in a
     Building Block Framework
     Jonas Svensson   82

7   Computing Consilience:
     How Modelling and Simulation can Contribute to
     Worldview Studies
     F. LeRon Shults   101

8 Comments and Reflections
  Ann Taves and Egil Asprem   113

  Index   126

Preface

Göran Larsson
University of Gothenburg

Andreas Nordin
University of Gothenburg

Jonas Svensson
Linnaeus University

The idea for the workshop, where all but one of the chapters of this volume were first presented in draft form, emerged from a discussion between the editors over why academics in Sweden have been comparatively slow in responding to suggestions that the sciences and the humanities should be integrated equally into the study of religions. This may be exemplified by the mere handful of researchers who have displayed any interest in the cognitive science of religion, despite the fact that it has been on the international agenda for almost 30 years. In the course of the discussion, Ann Taves was mentioned as a researcher who, though well-grounded in the humanistic study of religions, had nevertheless stressed the need for, in her own words, "fostering collaboration between the academic study of religion and the sciences" (Taves 2010) within the framework of a building block approach to religion.

We considered that arranging an academic workshop on this approach would be fruitful. Ann Taves was invited and accepted, on the condition that she could present her views together with Egil Aprem, with whom she had collaborated on the topic. Invitations were sent out to a small group of colleagues in Scandinavia all of whom we anticipated could contribute to the discussion from diverse fields within the study of religions. The workshop was held at Teleborg Castle in Växjö in June 2018. It was hosted by Linnaeus University and was made possible through generous funding from the Linnaeus University Centre for Concurrences in Colonial and Post-Colonial Studies.

About the Editors

Göran Larsson is a Professor in the study of religions at the University of Gothenburg. His main research focus is Islam and Muslims in Europe, both past and present, but he also has a general interest in theoretical and methodological questions concerning the study of humans, especially with regard to religion. Besides these topics, Larsson has also conducted research on global conflicts and how they impact on Swedish society. He has published several books, chapters and articles with international publishing houses, for example, Brill, Routledge, Springer, and Ashgate.

Andreas Nordin has a PhD in social anthropology, is an Associate Professor of Religious Studies, and a Lecturer in the Department of Cultural Sciences, University of Gothenburg, Sweden. Nordin's primary areas of research interest are cognitive and evolutionary anthropology, moral psychology, honour and reputation, religious cognition, and the cognitive science of religion.

Jonas Svensson is a professor in the study of religions at Linnaeus University. He specializes in Islamic studies, and has of late taken a particular interest in integrating the cognitive science of religion into his research field, as well as in ways in which to utilize computers and programming in humanistic research.

Reference

Taves, Ann. 2010. "No Field is an Island: Fostering Collaboration between the Academic Study of Religion and the Sciences." *Method and Theory in the Study of Religion* 22: 170–88.

By Way of Introduction

Göran Larsson
University of Gothenburg

Andreas Nordin
University of Gothenburg

Jonas Svensson
Linnaeus University

The building block approach (BBA) to the study of religions and worldviews suggested by Ann Taves (Santa Barbara University) and Egil Asprem (Stockholm University) can be seen as a more generally accessible formulation of a larger research program aimed at integrating the sciences and the humanities, often considered "two cultures" in academia. The intellectual grounding of the BBA is shared with a large number of scholars who belong to particular subdivisions of the study of religions, such as the cognitive and evolutionary science of religion and related fields in cognitive anthropology. Indeed, there is a sense in which scholars from these subfields may view the approach as "pushing at an open door". Nonetheless, we believe that there is indeed a need for more general formulation of the actual underlying research agenda, not least for the purposes of facilitating communication. For example, the editors of this volume have all encountered ambivalence among colleagues towards the above-mentioned approaches to the study of religions. We have chosen to interpret this attitude as a reluctance not to embracing the idea of inter-disciplinarity as such, but to the use of "scientistic" language. There may be a need for a less intimidating vocabulary, avoiding such technical terms as "mental modules", "behavioural scripts", or "Baysean predictive coding mechanisms in human perception". The metaphor of "building blocks" may just do the trick.

Could such an approach help in bridging this gap between the humanities and the natural sciences? Is such bridging necessary, or even desirable, given the general philosophy of science in our studies and its epistemological background? Is the call for "conciliation" and "vertical integration" in the scientific community that underlies the BBA legitimate, or is it merely a covert attempt at academic colonization that threatens the integrity of the humanities as a unique approach to the study of human culture, one focused on interpretation rather than explanation?

In the light of this brief backdrop, the aim of the following collection of texts is twofold. First, we wish to provide a short and user-friendly introduction to the approach formulated by Taves and Asprem. Secondly, we aim to offer a set of responses, discussions and possible applications relating to this approach. Hopefully, we will have inspired some researchers to pursue its adoption. Another possibility is that we have provoked some scholars to write responses and to sharpen their criticisms. Although we hope for the first response, we also think that all good scientific research is based on critical discussions and debates. Any response will help us to advance the study of religions, things deemed to be religious and other special things, as Taves usually puts it.

As a starting point for this volume, we asked Taves and Asprem to provide a background to how and when the BBA was developed and why they thought it necessary to develop this way of thinking about religion. To put it differently, what kinds of questions does their approach answer and what kinds of gaps in earlier research does it fill? Although this brought several difficult questions into the discussion, we asked Taves and Asprem to keep the introduction short, simple and as user-friendly as possible. For those who are interested a more elaborate presentation of the BBA is available in Taves' own book, *Religious Experience Reconsidered: A Building-Block Approach to the Study of Religion and Other Special Things* (Princeton, 2009; reprinted in 2011). This provides the necessary scientific background to the BBA and shows how it relates to earlier research and to other scientific fields, especially the cognitive science of religion and evolutionary studies of religions.

Disposition and Outline

The volume opens with an introduction by Taves and Asprem, followed by six responses to the BBA and suggestions for its application.

The introduction is followed by Göran Larsson's chapter, which provides an overview and assessment of how Taves' and Asprem's theoretical and methodological suggestions have been received by the academic community. The aim of Larsson's chapter is to help the reader who is encountering the BBA for the first time to assess the pros and cons that have been identified by other researchers. Furthermore, Larsson aims to show how difficult it is to bridge the gaps that exist between different philosophies of science in academia and why it is so difficult to achieve conciliation.

Laura Feldt's chapter does not test the BBA or use it as such. Instead her chapter questions and discusses the BBA from the perspective of the broader study of religion, focusing especially on the role of the media, materiality, and emotions, in the investigation of fantastic stories in ancient religions such the Mesopotamian, as well as contemporarily, in studies of religion and popular culture. Feldt encourages further discussion in the general study of religions between specialists in the cognitive science of religion and other historians of religion.

In his chapter, Andreas Nordin discusses the BBA from the perspective of some common standard methodological assumptions in the broader subfield of the cognitive and evolutionary science of religion and cognitive anthropology that suggest a piecemeal and "fractionated" understanding of so-called religious phenomena. This topic is addressed by defending the notion that the cognition of supernatural dreaming is a pervasive part and consequently a building block of religious experience and tradition.

Ingela Visuri's chapter presents an empirical and methodological example of an interdisciplinary study of religious cognition that is closely aligned to the BBA suggested by Taves and Asprem. While autism is the focal point of Visuri's research, the chapter also highlights a generational shift in the ascription of non-ordinary powers, which in these millennials appears to depart from occult phenomena in Western popular culture. Visuri argues that this cultural and temporal influence on religious cognition surfaces due to the mixing of methods and scientific approaches, and that such interdisciplinary designs enable researchers to observe a single phenomenon from multiple perspectives.

Jonas Svensson's chapter is an attempt to explore the usefulness of the BBA to the study of Islam by applying a theory of a building block type (Moral Foundations Theory) to a topic that falls well within the classical boundaries of the study of religions, namely Qur'an translations. Utilizing methods developed elsewhere to quantify moral foundations in texts with the help of computers, Svensson searches for possible patterns in the translations and considers how these patterns may be related to previous, ongoing, and future research within the field of Islamic studies.

F. LeRon Shults's chapter focuses on the second main problem the BBA was designed to solve – achieving conciliation – and the role that reverse engineering and predictive processing are supposed to play in fulfilling this transdisciplinary task. Shults argues that one of the best ways of analysing and explaining "complex cultural phenomena in terms of the constituent parts that interact to produce them" (p. 101) is provided by new techniques in computer modelling and simulation. The overall goal is to describe some of the ways in which these methodological tools can contribute to Taves' and Asprem's call for epistemological bridges to be constructed between the sciences and the humanities.

The volume ends with a chapter giving Taves and Asprem the opportunity to respond to the responses, applications, and suggestions presented in this book.

All the chapters described above have been written by scholars from Norway, Denmark, and Sweden. The restrictions on this selection are due to the composition of the initial workshop venue where draft versions of the final chapters were presented, except for F. LeRon Shults's text, which was added later. We nonetheless hope that the book may serve as an introduction for a wider audience in both Europe and North America, stimulating further debate, responses and critical discussion.

About the Editors

Göran Larsson is a Professor in the study of religions at the University of Gothenburg. His main research focus is Islam and Muslims in Europe, both past and present, but he also has a general interest in theoretical and methodological questions concerning the study of humans, especially with regard to religion. Besides these topics, Larsson has also conducted research on global conflicts and how they impact on Swedish society. He has published several books, chapters and articles with international publishing houses, for example, Brill, Routledge, Springer, and Ashgate.

Andreas Nordin has a PhD in social anthropology, is an Associate Professor of Religious Studies, and a Lecturer in the Department of Cultural Sciences, University of Gothenburg, Sweden. Nordin's primary areas of research interest are cognitive and evolutionary anthropology, moral psychology, honour and reputation, religious cognition, and the cognitive science of religion.

Jonas Svensson is a professor in the study of religions at Linnaeus University. He specializes in Islamic studies, and has of late taken a particular interest in integrating the cognitive science of religion into his research field, as well as in ways in which to utilize computers and programming in humanistic research.

1

The Building Block Approach: An Overview

Ann Taves

University of California, CA

Egil Asprem

Stockholm University

Introducing the Building Block Approach: What is it, and which Problems Does it Seek to Solve?

What is it?
The building block approach (hereafter BBA) is a method for analysing – and explaining – complex cultural phenomena in terms of the constituent parts that interact to produce them. By *constituent parts*, we refer to all the cognitive, psychological, and biological processes that guide human interaction with the environment (natural, built, and social) from perception and affect to memorization, categorization, and strategizing. While many scholars of religion are likely to agree that culture cannot emerge apart from the biological organisms that create it, it is often far less clear how one can relate the cultural to the biological in a meaningful way. This has created a methodological chasm between the "holistic" appreciation of cultural complexity and the "reductionist" explanatory efforts of the natural sciences that we are attempting to bridge with our BBA. In particular, the approach is designed to solve two related questions: (1) what terminology should we use when analysing and explaining cultural phenomena (such as "religions"), and (2) how can we achieve consilience between natural, behavioural, and humanistic sciences? Or, to put it in epistemological terms, how can we bridge the divide between naturalists and constructionists?

The problem with the term "religion"
We respond to the terminology problem by distinguishing between what we call "complex cultural concepts" (CCCs) and "basic concepts"

(BCs). In doing so, we signal our agreement with constructionist scholars of religion who emphasize that (1) "religion" is constructed by discursive practices that are inseparable from power relations and contests over resources, and (2) that this means one has to start not with identifying "religious traditions" in the world, but rather with analysing the *discourses on* religion (e.g. Taira 2013: 39–40). The first step in the BBA, which we call "reverse engineering", is therefore to locate, analyse and disentangle the CCCs, including in their *scholarly* formations (that is, formal definitions and casual uses of the terms by scholars). The BBA enables us to redescribe specific phenomena enlisted under CCCs as *something* (a basic concept) that is appraised in more specific cultural terms. Doing so clarifies what we need to explain and draws connections with practices that are normally appraised under different CCCs. While some worry that doing so will undercut the study of religion as a discipline, we find it more important that it connects our work with research in other humanities and social scientific disciplines and more firmly establishes our subject's relevance.

Call for consilience
The BBA is committed to consilience between the natural, behavioural, and humanistic sciences. It is a method that allows us to go beyond the analysis of discourse to understand the mechanisms that produce cultural phenomena, while recognizing that explanations must be premised on careful, detailed analysis of what we hope to explain. Enhancing this understanding of explanation as dependent on the careful "reverse engineering" of CCCs is one of our major goals (see Asprem and Taves 2018; Taves and Asprem, in preparation). Having a procedure for moving between the CCCs and more "basic concepts", which can be operationalized in precise terms in naturalistic and behavioural sciences, is a necessary step toward a better integration of, or consilience between, the humanities and the sciences. The aim is to provide a common language that allows scholars in the humanities and social sciences to bring psychological and neuroscientific research to bear on the phenomena they are studying. In this chapter, we will give an overview of some of the key concepts of this approach, how we got to them, and hint at how it can be applied in concrete research projects.

How did we come up with it?
This general statement of what we mean by a BBA first emerged through Ann Taves' reflection on problems surrounding the study of religious experience in *Religious Experience Reconsidered* (RER) (Taves 2011, originally published in 2009). The central argument of the book was that we should take an attributional approach in which we analyse "things

deemed religious" rather than "religious experience". This attributional formulation forces us to consider two interrelated issues: (1) the definition of "religious" and (2) who is doing the deeming – researchers or those who are recounting the experience. Initially, the plan for RER was to adopt a second order definition, which would have meant that Ann, as a researcher, was deeming some things as "religious". As Ann has often recounted, she gave up the idea when she realized that Jesper Sørensen's definition of magic and her proposed definition of religion were interchangeable (pp. 148–49, 161–63). Thus, in the final version, she concluded the overlap in scholarly definitions of supposedly different CCCs, such as religious, magical, and sacred, made their continued use as second order terms difficult, if not impossible.

Reflecting on who was doing the "deeming" highlighted the distinction between scholarly definitions, which function as attributions, and the appraisals of those recounting the experiences. This generated two separate lines of inquiry: (1) an analysis of definitions of religion and related terms, which led to refinements in our terminology and integration of the BBA with work on explanation, and (2) a more in-depth look at both appraisal processes and what was being appraised. We now view appraisal processes in terms of multiple levels of mechanisms and contend that experiences can be better understood as a type of *event* and religions as a type of *worldview*.

Examples: reverse engineering "religion" and "esotericism"
In the wake of RER, Ann published two articles (Taves 2013, 2015) that took apart scholarly definitions of religion and other related terms to specify more precisely what features the definitions were attributing to things when characterizing them as religious, sacred, and so on. Taking apart these definitions – or "reverse engineering" them – involved distinguishing between a generic phenomenon (a noun) and the feature that was attributed to it (for a summary, see Taves 2015: 196–97). In 2013, Egil Asprem began a two-year postdoctoral fellowship at UC Santa Barbara with the idea of applying this approach to the concept of esotericism.

Building on Ann's work on "religion" (Taves 2015), Egil reverse engineered the CCC "esotericism" as it appears in the academic study of esotericism (Asprem 2016). Following an attributional approach, he analysed the nouns (i.e. concepts) modified by the adjective "esoteric" in the 344 articles contained in the flagship *Dictionary of Gnosis and Western Esotericism*. He found that 42.4% of the concepts could be subsumed under the category of "knowledge" (e.g. ideas, teachings, truth, wisdom), while the majority of the other concepts deemed esoteric were historical trajectories or social formations that carry such knowledge (e.g. traditions, currents, schools, groups). This is to say that for scholars of esotericism, "esoteric" implicitly refers to a certain type of "knowledge" and the institutional and material vehicles for this knowledge. What makes some knowledge esoteric is, however, another question. Here, Egil showed that the specialist literature can be broken down into five definitional clusters that each point to separate qualities or processes that makes the knowledge esoteric. For example, knowledge can be deemed esoteric because (1) it is related to *secrecy*, (2) it is premised on an ostensibly special "form of thought" or "mentality" (typically emphasizing the "imagination" or "correspondences"), or (3) it has been *rejected* and *displaced* by other formations that view it as "improper" knowledge (e.g. as a form of heterodoxy).

During this phase, our aim was to highlight the wide range of things (e.g. experiences, powers, knowledge, agents, searches, concerns, etc.) to which the features could be attributed and to specify the features themselves more precisely. In specifying the features, we were able to identify basic cognitive abilities that humans rely upon when appraising situations and events and thus for ascribing the features to things. This laid the foundation for conceiving the processes not only in neurocognitive terms, but also for viewing them in an evolutionary perspective, that is, in relation to the abilities of humans and other animals.

In the process of taking apart these definitions, we generated more precise language to discuss the BBA and started integrating the BBA with work on explanation. This led us to reconceptualize the BBA in light of a recent school in the philosophy of science known as the New Mechanism, in which a mechanism is understood as explaining how the components of a system interact to produce or maintain the behaviour of that system. This definition was congruent with our understanding of the BBA, as seeking to understand, or explain, complex cultural phenomena through the constituent parts that make them work and, at the same time, allowed us to embed our focus on complex cultural phenomena in a multi-level explanatory framework. Our Building Blocks of Human Experience website (Asprem and Taves 2016) reflects this new line of thinking about the BBA as does our co-authored work on explanation (Asprem and Taves 2018; Taves and Asprem in preparation).

Appraisal processes and things appraised

While we were taking apart scholarly definitions, we were also working with historical materials to analyse how those who had unusual experiences appraised them. Building on the social psychological analysis in RER, we more fully integrated lines of research on appraisal processes drawn from sociology, cognitive psychology, and neuroscience to generate a more complex multi-level understanding. This multi-level approach was informed both by the new mechanistic understanding of explanation and our realization that experiences can be viewed as events and thus

> **Definitions**
> Source: Building Blocks of Human Experience Website (Asprem and Taves, 2016)
>
> Reverse Engineering is the research strategy at the heart of the BBA. Simply put, reverse engineering entails a series of steps designed to take apart a complex system and analyse its constituent parts in order to (1) find out how it works and (2) trace how the parts (events, actions, and representations) have been assembled and labelled in specific formations. It thus is the basic strategy for learning more about human experience as it is mediated by CCCs and social formations.
>
> Complex Cultural Concepts (CCCs) are abstract nouns with unstable, overlapping meanings that vary within and across social formations. Their adjectival forms can be used to characterize generic things, like experiences, practices, objects, and so on. Terms like "religious", "spiritual", "hallucinatory", "sacred", "revelatory", "occult", "heretical", "superstitious", "magical", and "delusional" are examples of adjectivized CCCs. We contrast them with Basic Concepts.
>
> Basic Concepts (BCs) are concepts that translate relatively easily across formations and levels because they refer to broadly shared aspects of human experience, rooted in embodied interactions with the environment and evolved mental architecture shared by the entire species. Examples include the embodied metaphors and image-schemata discussed in cognitive linguistics (e.g. path, containment, back-front), as well as concepts like events, actions, and representations. Rendering the various *denotations* of CCCs in generic, basic concepts is essential for the development of fine-grained and precise analyses and fair, unbiased comparisons across formations.
>
> A Social Formation is any entity (organization, movement, network) that links persons in a way that stabilizes terminology and meanings through shared discourse and practice. Examples of formations include religions, traditions, political movements, social networks, and academic disciplines. Insofar as CCCs are built into formations, they typically take on specialized meanings within and for those formations.
>
> Mechanism: The BBA rests on an influential current in recent philosophy of science known as "the new mechanical philosophy", or "the new mechanism" (see Craver and Tabery 2015). In this framework, a mechanism explains the behaviour of a phenomenon in terms of the interaction of parts, also referred to as components or building blocks. Thus, "[a] mechanism for a phenomenon consists of entities (or parts) whose activities and interactions are organized in such a way that they produce the phenomenon" (Glennan 2015).

analysed in light of recent work on event cognition (Taves and Asprem 2017). These developments were integrated into our historical work (see Taves 2016a and Asprem 2017).

Just as there was a specific moment when Taves gave up defining religion, so too there was a specific moment when she realized she had to take the next step and identify the larger class of things in which religion/s (however conceived) belonged. This moment came in 2016 in response to an invitation to write a blog post on how concepts and theories from religious studies could be applied to the study of nonreligion and secularity. In contrast to the invitation's hopeful focus on borrowing, she felt that the extension of concepts from the study of religion to nonreligion pushed our already troubled concepts to breaking point. If we could not define religion, how could we possibly define nonreligion? At the same time, the juxtaposition of religion and nonreligion made it obvious that both were examples of *something*, without specifying what that something was. The juxtaposition, in other words, surfaced a tacit comparison between religion and nonreligion without specifying the point of analogy between them. It was, she said, "as if we set out to compare apples and oranges without realizing that they [were] both fruits".

In the blog post and two invited lectures in which she was asked to extend her research on experience into secular educational and clinical contexts (Taves 2016b; 2018a; 2018b), she began discussing the larger framework in light of research on meaning systems in psychology and worldviews in the humanities. In the wake of the 2016 lectures, we have been developing the idea of religions as worldviews in a series of articles (Taves and Asprem 2018; Taves, Asprem, and Ihm 2018), in the Gunning Lectures[1] (given in Edinburgh, March 2018), and at the Conference on Future Directions in the Evolution of Religion (Erice, Italy, April 2018).

Theoretical Underpinnings and Influences

Epistemological foundation: a critical naturalistic constructionism

The problems we have discussed so far – the status of "religion" and consilience between the humanities and the natural sciences – require us to address more fundamental epistemological questions. One way to frame the issue is through the distinction between constructionist positions, which stress that scientific knowledge is produced socially and culturally and on that ground remain sceptical about claims to "reality", and

---

1. These three lectures, "The Gunning Lectures on Worldviews and Ways of Life", constitute the most in-depth explication of the approach to date. The lectures were titled: (1) Studying Religion/s as Worldviews and Ways of Life, (2) The Evolutionary Foundations of Worldviews, (3) The Emergence of New Worldviews and Ways of Life.

naturalistic positions, which view science as an activity that seeks knowledge about "natural kinds" existing independently of humans knowing them (cf. Bird and Tobin 2018; *Stanford Encyclopedia of Philosophy*, "Natural Kinds"). While this distinction is often discussed in absolute terms, it is perfectly possible to take a constructionist position on some things and a realist position on others. Our stance on "religion" is a case in point. We think that constructionists are right that religion is a social construct that does not exist independently of people appraising certain phenomena as such. Yet, we remain naturalists at base. In the language of naturalism, we propose that religion is *not a natural kind*. At the same time, however, the BBA is based on the view that natural kinds *do* exist, and that the many diverse phenomena that get appraised as "religion" are built from the interaction of such natural kinds. For example, the human ability to infer the intentions and mental states of others (often called Theory of Mind in evolutionary psychology) is a natural kind that has developed over the course of evolution. It is also widely considered a building block of "religion" insofar as "religion" is construed in terms of intentional non- and super-human agents and the evolved mental capacity to infer the mind of others extended to them.

Our position can be described as a critical, qualified constructionism on naturalistic grounds (Asprem 2014: 81–84). It borrows from constructionism the view that articulated cultural systems such as religions, moral norms, or philosophies are constructed through the interplay of human social actors, and that socialization thus plays a major role in their emergence and development. At the same time, it emphasizes that language and socialization itself are made possible by evolved capacities that exist independently of whether we know about them, how we name them, and what we think about them. It is from this double-sided position that we think consilience between the humanities and the natural sciences must spring. The interdisciplinary knowledge that we seek must be able to qualitatively assess the particulars of cultural phenomena, on the one hand, and relate the variations and stable features of culture across populations of humans and non-human animals alike, on the other. It is from this critical naturalist position that we orient ourselves in the recent philosophy of science literature and pay especially close attention to philosophical positions developed in the context of the life sciences.

Theoretical schools that have influenced us

The approach has led us to a wide range of theoretical schools. Here we will focus on those that have been most central to the development of the approach: the new mechanism in philosophy of science, and scientific research on appraisal processes and event cognition.

New mechanism: building blocks as components of mechanisms

We are now grounding the BBA theoretically in an influential current in recent philosophy of science known as "the new mechanical philosophy", or "the new mechanism" (see Craver and Tabery 2016; Glennan and Illari 2017). In this framework, a mechanism *explains* the behaviour of a phenomenon in terms of the interaction of parts, which we also refer to as components or building blocks. Thus, "[a] mechanism for a phenomenon consists of entities (or parts) whose activities and interactions are organized in such a way that they produce the phenomenon" (Glennan 2015). "The new mechanists" are developing this approach to explanation based on how research is done in the so-called "special sciences", such as biology and neuroscience, which focus on biological organisms. In our current work on explanation (Taves and Asprem, in preparation), we are drawing on recent work in the social sciences (Ylikoski 2012, 2013, 2014; Kaiser *et al.* 2014) to extend this approach from biological organisms to the human sociocultural phenomena studied by scholars in the humanities with a particular focus on the role of human intention in the making of shared (cultural) worlds.

The approach to explanation promoted by the new mechanists assumes the importance of careful analytical descriptions of the phenomenon of interest prior to any attempt to explain the building blocks or components that interact to explain the phenomenon. Their approach parallels that advocated by philosopher of religion, Wayne Proudfoot (1985), who distinguished between descriptive reduction (redescribing the phenomenon in ways that subjects would be unable to recognize), which he viewed as problematic, and explanatory reduction (explaining the phenomenon in terms unfamiliar to the subjects), which he argued was legitimate. We have long been convinced by Proudfoot's distinction, which we presuppose as historians and carry over into our work on explanation.

Although humanists generally focus on phenomena at the level of human behaviour, phenomena of interest can be located at any scale from particles to cells to organisms to societies, depending on the interests of the researchers. The components that explain the phenomenon of interest to one researcher may be the phenomenon of interest to another researcher. Each component, thus, may be a phenomenon of interest, produced by the interaction of its own set of components. Mechanisms are thus nested in synchronic "stacks". Mechanisms may also be lined up diachronically to allow us to explain chains of events. Here too the researcher selects the scale at which they describe the chain of events and, thus, the level of mechanism that will explain it.

Deeming as an appraisal process
The attributional approach advocated in RER drew heavily on attribution theory as developed within social psychology (see Taves 2011: 88–119, with particular reliance on the work of Malle 2004). We are now using "appraisal processes" as an umbrella term that encompasses research on appraisal processes in neuroscience (e.g. Ashar, Chang, and Wager 2017) and psychology (e.g. Lazarus and Folkman 1984; Scherer, Schorr, and Johnstone 2001), attribution theory in social psychology, and framing processes in sociology (e.g. Goffman 1974; Benford and Snow 2000). As an umbrella term, we use it to refer to the multi-level processes that humans and other animals rely on when determining what is happening, that is, to interpret situations and events. Deeming, attributing, and ascribing are terms that are generally used to refer to the more conscious levels of the appraisal process. In the cognitive sciences (including cognitive anthropology), terms such as schemas, scripts, and cultural models are used to refer to unconscious appraisals (for an overview, see Bennardo and DeMunck 2014: 37–56).

Experiences as events
In RER, the distinction between "experience" in the abstract and "an experience" was not characterized with any precision. With the discovery of the research on event cognition (Zacks and Tversky 2001; Zacks et al. 2007; Radvansky and Zacks 2011, 2014), we were able to conceptualize both more precisely. Based on the definition of an "event" as "a segment of time at a given location that is conceived by an observer to have a beginning and an end" (Zacks and Tversky 2001: 3), we were able to specify "experience" as the flow of information insofar as we are aware of it and "an experience" as a discrete event that has been segmented out of the flow of experience such that it is perceived to have a beginning and an end (see Taves and Asprem 2017).

Psychologically, event cognition refers to a set of mechanisms that allow us not only to form mental representations of what is going on around us and segment it into discrete, bounded events, but also to identify and store knowledge about specific types of events, predict what will happen next, and use these models to regulate action – from basic motor control to complex intentional action sequences (Radvansky and Zacks 2014). As a subpersonal process, it takes place (for the most part) below the threshold of consciousness. Internalized schemas and input from bottom-up signals from our body and the environment are the key components that interact to produce our sense of "what's happening". Event cognition, thus, provides a mechanism that (a) constitutes an event as such, (b) identifies components (i.e. information from the body and the environment, event schemas, and memories of specific past events) that interact to allow humans and other more highly evolved animals to predict what is happening, and (c) act in accord with their predictions. Research on event cognition, which is at the cutting edge of current cognitive science, now forms the foundation that links our cross-cultural work on experience, our historical analysis of narratives and practice traditions, and our evolutionary perspectives on worldviews and ways of life (see below).[2]

> Experience is the flow of information insofar as we are aware of it.
>
> An Experience (Erlebnis) is a discrete event that has been segmented out of the flow of experience such that it is perceived to have a beginning and an end. Phenomenologically, "experiences" are personally experienced events that are particularly salient.
>
> Lived Experience encompasses behaviours (perceiving, doing, feeling) and events (happenings) that people are aware of, whether individually or collectively.
>
> Accumulated Experience (Erfahrung) refers to being experienced, having proficiency in a domain.

Experience. In contrast to constructivist approaches to religious experience, which tend to assume that appraisals are only made after the fact, and perennialist approaches, which tend to assume that (some) experiences are not appraised, we draw on the research on event cognition to understand how stimuli can be unconsciously appraised while the experience is occurring. This research suggests that we draw unconsciously on learned cultural schemas, which we may acquire through observation, participation, or intensive practice, to generate working models of what is happening (what we are experiencing) while it is occurring. Insofar as what we have learned is stored in memory as schemas and drawn upon unconsciously to model what is happening in the context of the experience itself, we can acknowledge the perennialist claim that they did not consciously interpret their experience without essentializing it. This research also suggests that learned cultural schemas will influence the frequency and clustering of experiences in different cultural contexts, a hypothesis we are currently testing using our Inventory of Nonordinary Experiences (see below).

---

2. Portions of this and the preceding paragraph were taken from Taves and Asprem 2017.

Narrative. In the light of this research, we can view the narration of our experiences as events in their own right, derived from our memory of the mental models we generated in the context of the experience itself. Our memory of past events is partial and selective, typically attuned to the new context in which the experience is remembered and/or recounted. Thus, as the constructionists claim, people definitely do appraise and reappraise their experiences after the fact as they reflect on what it meant. Where the primary sources are rich enough, historians may be able to track the way individuals or emergent groups interpreted and reinterpreted an event over time and in different contexts.

Training. The cultural schemas that inform our perceptions of events are typically learned through participation in everyday life and sometimes developed and more deeply internalized through more intensive practices. We are investigating the role of more intensive practices using historical methods (see below) and the Inventory (mentioned above).

Evolution. The human ability to make sense of events is highly developed, but like other human abilities rests on an evolutionary foundation. We are relying on the work of Merlin Donald (1993, 2002) to understand the evolutionary development of the human ability to cognize events, because they lie at the heart of his understanding of the evolution of human consciousness. While complex mammals can chunk the flow of information into discrete events with a beginning and an end and non-human primates can recall events based on environmental cues, humans add to this the ability to voluntarily recall events, which they can interpret based on cultural, as well as evolved, event schemas. We are using this and other research on human cultural evolution in our current work, which locates religion/s as an aspect of ways of life and, in some cases, a species of worldview (see current and future work).

Applications

Studying experience across cultures

We can take a BBA to both named kinds (clusters) of experiences and accounts of particular experiences, treating named clusters of experiences as CCCs and accounts of particular experiences as events. Named kinds of experiences are clusters of experiences that people have placed under a common label. The clusters may be broadly conceived as (e.g.) religious, spiritual, mystical, paranormal, occult, or psychotic experiences or more narrowly conceived as (e.g.) spirit possession, astral projection, or apparitions. In either case, we find that phenomenologically distinct experiences may be clustered under a common label and that phenomenologically similar experiences may appear under different labels. For example, mystical experience has been associated historically with a range of phenomenologically distinct experiences. The same can be said of astral projection. Alternatively the sense that the self has left the body can occur in the context of sleep paralysis, near death experience, shamanism, and astral travel. Given this, we cannot assume that named clusters of experiences refer to cross-culturally stable natural kinds, but must be alert to the possibility that experiences are clustered in light of CCCs specific to particular communities of thought and practice. In such cases, the CCCs function to simultaneously cluster and distinguish experiences in accordance with the values and commitments of the community. So, for example, some communities define mystical experiences in terms of experiences of unity and explicitly exclude visionary experience, even though the two often occur together in practice. We refer to these communities of discourse generically as Social Formations and include under that heading a wide range of organizations, movements, and networks, including religious traditions and academic disciplines.

To test whether these experiences fall into stable clusters, Taves and colleagues have constructed an Inventory of Nonordinary Experiences, in which they treat the experiences included in the various measures as independent items, regardless of whether the measures were designed to assess religious, anomalous, or psychiatric experiences (Taves, Kinsella and Barlev, unpublished). Items were re-grouped based on their phenomenological characteristics and stripped of appraisals to create descriptions that are as generic as possible, for example, "I have had an experience in which it seemed as if I had left my body". After participants indicate whether they have had each of the 80 experiences, they are asked follow-up questions about the context and the way they appraised the experiences they reported having had, for example, "When it was occurring, how did it feel?", "How, if at all, has it affected your life?", "What do you believe caused it?", and "Do you consider it religious or spiritual?". Following the inventory, participants answer demographic and individual difference questions regarding their religious/spiritual identification(s) and practice.

Distinguishing between the generic experience and the appraisal illustrates the decompositional phase in which we take experiences apart in order to better understand how components interact to produce the individual's recounted experience. If the frequency and clustering of experiences differs between cultures and traditions, it will provide evidence of underlying cultural schemas that are generating differences. This is the constructive phase of the BBA.

Revelatory events

A BBA to experiences not only allows us to make more nuanced comparisons across cultures, it also allows us to track the interpretation of experiences by individuals and groups over time. In some cases, groups coalesce around a particular interpretation of a real or imagined event. The Abrahamic traditions, for example, coalesced around accounts of events that they viewed as revelatory. Thus, early Christians coalesced around the claim that Jesus was the Messiah, rabbinic Jews around the claim that YHWH revealed both the oral and written Torah to Moses on Sinai, and Muslims around the claim that Allah revealed the Qur'an through his Prophet Muhammad. These traditions were new social formations, each of which was constituted through a collective appraisal of a past or present event (what ostensibly happened on Sinai, who Jesus was thought to be, or the alleged source of the words spoken by Muhammad). In each case, others disagreed. Generally speaking, groups are constituted by agreements regarding how a thing (an object, event, action, person, etc.) should be appraised and by performing behaviours that support the appraisal. These agreements simultaneously constitute the thing (the object, event, action, person) and the group. The BBA can, thus, be used to reconstruct the role of collective appraisals in the emergence of new social formations.

In *Revelatory Events* (Taves 2016a), Taves reconstructed the emergence of three new, relatively well-documented spiritual paths – Mormonism, Alcoholics Anonymous, and *A Course in Miracles* – and sought to explain how each came to view its emergence as guided by a supernatural presence. The book is divided into two parts. The first part, comprised of three chapters per group, is devoted to a detailed historical analysis of the emergence of the groups that attempts to reconstruct the interactive interpretive process as it unfolded in real time. Establishing this required working with the best available real-time sources and analysing post-hoc narratives in light of the later contexts in which they were produced. In analysing event narratives, she distinguished between the experiencers' perceptions (what happened) and appraisals (their implicit or explicit explanations of why it happened). When sources permitted, she compared multiple accounts of a single event to see how a subject reinterpreted it over time and multiple versions of a more comprehensive narrative (an event series) to analyse the way the narrator positioned a particular event within a larger narrative framework. This careful analytical work allowed her to identify similarities and differences in how the small groups formed in relation to the unusual experiences of the key figures. In the second part, she sought to explain the emergence of these new spiritual paths, the alleged presences that guided the process, and the production of the scripture-like texts in naturalistic terms. Doing so required her to account for three main things: (1) how people came to believe that a presence other than themselves was acting in their midst, (2) how this presence was able not only to guide, but especially in the case of the Book of Mormon and the Course in Miracles, to produce complex texts, and (3) who or what the presences were and what motivated believers (but not sceptics) to credit them with revealing the texts and the paths.

Esoteric practices

A BBA to experiences has also allowed us to highlight how particular kinds of experiences and ascriptions are cultivated in particular traditions through practice. Asprem (2017) has proposed that the common focus in Western esotericism on cultivating the "imagination" in order to gain knowledge from visions, dreams, and voices can be understood through specific neurocognitive mechanisms that exploit the perceptual systems' reliance on making inferences about what is happening. He proposes a mechanism by which individual psychological differences, skill development through repeated attentional practices, cultural schemata for culturally salient events, and enactive engagements with material objects that yield specific sensory stimuli are all linked together as components that interact to produce "kataphatic practice".

But, and this is the key comparative point, kataphatic practices that involve the cultivation of imagination are not limited to groups deemed "esoteric". By focusing on the practices that certain groups associate with "special knowledge", we can identify underlying processes (e.g. conceptual blending or cultivation of the imagination) that are used by many other groups as well, and for different purposes. By distinguishing between CCCs and more basic concepts we thus can arrive at (1) mechanistic explanations of *how specific practices work* through the interaction of component parts (building blocks), and (2) explanations that cover a broader set of practices than those of the specific social formation we study.

Worldviews and ways of life

In recent work, we are arguing that the unstable CCC "religion" might be framed positively as a subset of the more generic concepts of worldviews and ways of life. We are treating formal, systematized "religions" – however defined – as worldviews and the vague, abstract concept of "religion" as an aspect of ways of life. In a series of papers and lectures (see Taves and Asprem 2018; Taves, Asprem, and Ihm 2018), we define worldviews as a complex set of representations related to the "big questions" (BQs) that define and govern a way of life.

Although there is room for variation, we have adapted our formulation of the BQs from the Worldviews Research Group (Vidal 2008) founded by

Leo Apostel, now centred at the Free University in Brussels,[3] and the work of cultural anthropologist, André Droogers (2014), now retired from the Free University in Amsterdam. They are as follows:

1. What exists, what is real? (Ontology)
2. Who are we, where do we come from and where are we going? (Cosmology)
3. How do we know what is true? (Epistemology)
4. What is the situation in which we find ourselves? What is our nature? (Situation)
5. What is the good (or goal) that we should strive for? (Axiology)
6. What actions should we take? What path should we follow? (Praxeology)

While the BQs are usually understood as questions that philosophers, scientists, and theologians spend their lives pondering, we view them as much more basic than that. All organisms must have some representation of what its world is like, how it should react to different kinds of stimuli, and what stimuli are "good" and "bad" if it is to survive and thrive. In practice, answers to these questions are embedded in the organism's representations of itself and its environment (its world- and self-representations), which are themselves products of the organism's evolutionary history. We argue that the BQs are initially asked by natural selection itself and are, thus, implicit in an organism's way of life. The organism's way of life – its habitual patterns of interaction with affordances in its world – and its possibilities for interaction with its environment are premised on the nature and complexity of the organism's sensory and cognitive abilities. While all organisms have a way of life, we stipulate that only those who can *ask* as well as answer the BQs generate worldviews. Because, in this view, worldviews emerge from the ways of life in which they are embedded, they are typically enacted, articulated, and rationalized on a need-to-know basis. As a result, the articulated and coherent elaborations of worldviews associated with philosophy or theology are only the tip of an iceberg that reaches deep into evolutionary history.

Because worldviews, as we conceive them, emerge from ways of life, individuals, groups, and larger societies may express their worldviews in a variety of different ways at different times and in relation to different situations. For example:

---

3. See the websites of the Center Leo Apostel and the related Worldviews Research Group at http://www.vub.ac.be/CLEA/index.shtml and http://www.vub.ac.be/CLEA/dissemination/groups-archive/vzw_worldviews/

1. Aspects of a worldview can be enacted in practice. They are embedded in a way of life. Mostly taken-for-granted. Generally learned informally. They don't necessarily cohere.
2. Aspects of a worldview can be spoken. What is said may or may not reflect the enacted worldview. Articulation enables people to offer justifications for their behaviour.
3. Elements of a worldview can be memorized and recounted orally. This enables more formal teaching and empowers specialists.
4. Elements of a worldview may also be preserved in writing. Textualization enables systemization, rationalization, and commentary. Textualization enables the creation of highly systematized and rationalized worldviews, as well as attempts to promote them. But as we all know, these efforts succeed only in part.

In our ongoing work, we suspect that the biological foundations of worldviews and ways of life – their most fundamental building block – is found in a naturally occurring process known as "predictive processing", a computation-like modelling process which approximates Bayesian inferences and which is thought to be central to cognition as well as to natural selection itself (see, e.g., Clark 2016; Friston 2018). Since even the most basic and automatic representations of self-and-world are models *for* as well as models *of*, they only succeed to the extent that they are embedded in (probabilistic) answers to questions about what exists (ontology), what to move toward and against (axiology), and how to practically manoeuvre in their "world" of affordances (praxeology). Moreover, organisms "know" and adjust (epistemology) these answers through a Bayesian inference process where "prior probabilities" (in the shape of patterns of interaction or even phenotypical features) are gradually modified in light of new experience. Humans can update probabilities fairly quickly through learning; they are also updated – albeit slowly – through natural selection, where, as Carl Friston (2018) has suggested, each individual organism takes the role of a hypothesis that is tested against its niche. In the light of this, we have translated the BQs into language that is appropriate to evolution by natural selection and emerging work in predictive processing, as seen in the following table:

Insofar as our translation is persuasive, then worldviews – defined structurally in terms of BQs – are evolutionary elaborations of the BQs that are simultaneously embedded in and emerge out of human ways of life. Human answers to the BQs vary more widely than those of other species due to humans' heightened ability to cognize events, which includes the abilities to imagine events and generate shared representations of

Table 1: Big Questions in Language of Predictive Processing (based on Taves and Asprem 2018; Taves, Asprem, and Ihm 2018)

Ontology What exists?	Organisms with the capacity to select and appraise incoming information against top-down predictions (based in genetics and/or prior experience) and in doing so to generate self-and-world models.
Cosmology Who am I?	The organism's self-model provides an answer to the most basic cosmology question.
Ethology: What is the situation in which I find myself?	The organism's world-model provides an answer to the most basic situational question.
Axiology What is my goal? What is good and bad?	Ultimate preferences (good and bad) are built into the organism's world-and-self models through a natural selection of goals: organisms embodying models that strive for survival-enhancing uses of available affordances (food, mating, avoidance of predators and environmental dangers) prevail.
Praxeology What do I do? How do I act?	Best available actions in a situation are determined from an organism's best prediction of what is (ontology) in accord with the affordance-based goals and values embodied in its self-model (axiology).
Epistemology How do I know what is true about the world?	Organisms embody a Bayesian epistemology that constantly tests "what is true" through probability-based interactions with the environment constrained by survival pressures. Revising models can be very slow and often works on the population level rather than natural selection.

events. Taken together, these abilities enable humans to generate *shared, populations specific* ways of life governed by worldviews that they enact, articulate, recount, and reflect upon.

Structurally, worldviews can be understood as "natural kinds", in the sense of reflecting "the structure of the natural world rather than the interests and actions of human beings" (Bird and Tobin 2018; *Stanford Encyclopedia of Philosophy*, "Natural Kinds"). The same, however, cannot be said for their content, that is, for the specific answers that humans generate to the BQs; these we would maintain *do* reflect the specific interests and actions of human beings. Worldviews, thus, link the biological (natural) and the cultural (constructed) aspects of human life.

Future Directions

In the future, we want to develop the case for subsuming Religious Studies under the wider rubric of Critical Worldview Studies. We plan to elaborate on these basic points:

1. Defining worldviews in terms of BQs allows scholars of religious and other worldviews to position our interests in relation to others in the humanities and social sciences.
   (i) Relative to anthropology and cultural studies, it highlights the BQs as the aspect of culture of most interest to us.
   (ii) It enables us to study the worldviews of individuals and groups without requiring us to stipulate a boundary between religion and nonreligion, thus enabling us to explore the relationship between worldviews people characterize as religious, esoteric, imaginary, political, economic, and so on.
2. Approaching worldviews from an evolutionary perspective that highlights the BQs as basic questions that all organisms must answer grounds our research in a conciliant framework.
   (i) It allows us to conceive worldviews as embedded in ways of life and emerging on a need-to-know basis. An evolutionary approach upends top-down approaches that assume that the highly developed and systematized worldviews of philosophers and theologians are the standard from which "lived worldviews" have departed. It thus accounts for why "theologically incorrect" views are so resilient.
   (ii) The BQs offer a stable panhuman basis for comparison across cultures and a foundation for analysing how people express, elaborate, revise, and defend their worldviews, including the use they make of CCCs, such as religious, spiritual, and secular, in doing so.

About the Authors

Ann Taves is Distinguished Professor of religious studies at the University of California at Santa Barbara, Santa Barbara, CA.

Egil Asprem is Associate Professor of the history of religions at Stockholm University. His diverse research interests circle around the history of Western esotericism and new religious movements, with an emphasis on the implications of theoretical and methodological work in the social and cognitive sciences for these fields. His recent publications include *The Problem of Disenchantment: Scientific Naturalism and Esoteric Discourse* (Brill, 2014/SUNY, 2018) and the *Brill Handbook of Conspiracy Theory and Contemporary Religion* (Brill, 2018; co-edited with Asbjørn Dyrendal and David G. Robertson).

References

Ashar, Yoni K., Luke J. Chang, and Tor D. Wager. 2017. "Brain Mechanisms of the Placebo Effect: An Affective Appraisal Account." *Annual Review of Clinical Psychology* 13: 73–98.
Asprem, Egil. 2014. *The Problem of Disenchantment: Scientific Naturalism and Esoteric Discourse, 1900-1939.* Leiden: Brill.
—2016. "Reverse-Engineering 'Esotericism': How to Prepare a Complex Cultural Concept for the Cognitive Science of Religion." *Religion* 46(2): 158–85.
—2017. "Explaining the Esoteric Imagination: Towards a Theory of Kataphatic Practice." *Aries – Journal for the Study of Western Esotericism* 17(1): 17–50.
Asprem, Egil, and Ann Taves. 2016. "Building Blocks of Human Experience Website." Retrieved from: http://bbhe.ucsb.edu/ (accessed 7 May, 2018).
—2018. "Explanation and the Study of Religion." In *Method Today: Beyond Description and Hermeneutics in Religious Studies Scholarship*, edited by Brad Stoddard, 133–57. Sheffield: Equinox.
Benford, Robert. D., and David A. Snow. 2000. "Framing Processes and Social Movements: An Overview and Assessment." *Annual Review of Sociology* 26(1): 611–39.
Bennardo, Giovanni, and Victor C. DeMunck. 2014. *Cultural Models: Genesis, Methods, and Experiences.* New York: Oxford University Press.
Bird, Alexander, and Emma Tobin. 2018. "Natural Kinds." In *The Stanford Encyclopedia of Philosophy*, edited by Edward N. Zalta. Retrieved from https://plato.stanford.edu/archives/spr2018/entries/natural-kinds/
Clark, Andy. 2016. *Surfing Uncertainty: Prediction, Action, and the Embodied Mind.* New York: Oxford University Press.
Craver, Carl F., and James Tabery. 2016. "Mechanisms in Science." In *The Stanford Encyclopedia of Philosophy*, edited by Edward N. Zalta. Retrieved from: http://plato.stanford.edu/archives/spr2016/entries/science-mechanisms/
Donald, Merlin. 1993. "Précis of Origins of the Modern Mind: Three Stages in the Evolution of Culture and Cognition." *Behavioral and Brain Sciences* 16: 737–91.
—2002. *A Mind So Rare: The Evolution of Human Consciousness.* New York: Norton.
Droogers, André. F. 2014. "The World of Worldviews." In *Methods for the Study of Religious Change*, edited by André. F. Droogers and Anton van Harskamp, 17–42. London: Equinox.
Friston, Karl. 2018. "Am I Self-Conscious? (Or Does Self-Organization Entail Self-Consciousness?)." *Frontiers in Psychology* 9, 24 April. https://doi.org/10.3389/fpsyg.2018.00579
Glennan, Stuart. 2015. "Mechanisms and Mechanical Philosophy." In *The Oxford Handbook of Philosophy of Science*, edited by Paul Humphreys, 796–816. Oxford and New York: Oxford University Press.
Glennan, Stuart, and Phyllis Illari, eds. 2017. *The Routledge Handbook of Mechanisms and Mechanical Philosophy.* New York and London: Routledge.
Goffman, Erving. 1974. *Frame Analysis: An Essay on the Organization of Experience.* Cambridge, MA: Harvard University Press.
Kaiser, Marie I., Oliver R. Scholz, Daniel Plenge, and Andreas Hüttemann, eds. 2014. *Explanation in the Special Sciences: The Case of Biology and History.* Berlin: Springer.
Lazarus, Richard S., and Susan Folkman. 1984. *Stress, Appraisal, and Coping.* New York: Springer Publishing.

Malle, Bertram. F. 2004. *How the Mind Explains Behaviour: Folk Explanations, Meaning, and Social Interaction*. Cambridge: MIT Press.
Proudfoot, Wayne. 1985. *Religious Experience*. Berkeley: University of California Press.
Radvansky, Gabriel, and Jeffrey M. Zacks. 2011. "Event Perception." *Wiley Interdisciplinary Reviews: Cognitive Science* 2(6): 608–20.
—2014. *Event Cognition*. Oxford: Oxford University Press.
Scherer, Klaus. R., Angela Schorr, and Tom Johnstone, eds. 2001. *Appraisal Processes in Emotion: Theory, Methods, Research*. New York: Oxford University Press.
Taira, Teemu. 2013. "Making Space for Discursive Study in Religious Studies." *Religion* 43(1): 26–45.
Taves, Ann. 2011 [2009]. *Religious Experience Reconsidered: A Building Block Approach to the Study of Religion and Other Special Things*. Princeton, NJ: Princeton University Press.
—2013. "Building Blocks of Sacralities: A New Basis for Comparison across Cultures and Religions." In *Handbook of Psychology of Religion and Spirituality*, edited by Raymond F. Paloutzian and Crystal Park, 138–61. New York: Guilford Press.
—2015. "Reverse Engineering Complex Cultural Concepts: Identifying Building Blocks of Religion." *Journal of Cognition and Culture* 15(1-2): 191–216.
—2016a. *Revelatory Events: Three Case Studies of the Emergence of New Spiritual Paths*. Princeton, NJ: Princeton University Press.
—2016b. "On the Virtues of a Meaning Systems Framework for Studying Nonreligious and Religious Worldviews in the Context of Everyday Life." Published on *Nonreligion and Secularity Research Network blog*. Retrieved from: https://nsrn.net/2016/10/04/methods-series-on-thevirtues-of-a-meaning-systems-framework (revised and in press as "What is Nonreligion?").
—2018a. "Finding and Articulating Meaning in Secular Experience." In *Religious Experience and Experiencing Religion in Religious Education*, edited by Daniel Fleming, Eva-Maria Leven, and Ulrich Riegel, 13–22. München: Waxmann Verlag.
—2018b. "What is Nonreligion? On the Virtues of a Meaning Systems Framework for Studying Nonreligious and Religious Worldviews in the Context of Everyday Life." *Secularism and Nonreligion* 7(9): 1–6.
Taves, Ann, and Egil Asprem. 2017. "Experience as Event: Event Cognition and the Study of (Religious) Experience." *Religion, Brain & Behavior* 7: 43–62.
—2018. "Scientific Worldview Studies: A Programmatic Proposal." In *A New Synthesis: Cognition, Evolution, and History in the Study of Religion*, edited by Anders K. Petersen, Ingvild S. Gilhus, Luther H. Martin, Jeppe S. Jensen, and Jesper Sørensen. Leiden: Brill.
—In preparation. *Explanation: A Conceptual Primer*. London: Equinox.
Taves, Ann, Egil Asprem, and Elliot Ihm. 2018. "Psychology, Meaning Making and the Study of Worldviews: Beyond Religion and Nonreligion." *Psychology of Religion & Spirituality* 10(3): 207–17.
Taves, Ann, Michael Kinsella, and Michael Barlev. (unpublished). *The Inventory of Nonordinary Experiences*.
Vidal, Clément. 2008. "Wat is een wereldbeeld?" In *Nieuwheid denken*, edited by Hubert Van Belle and Jan Van der Veken, 71–86. Leuven: Acco.
Ylikoski, Petri. 2012. "Micro, Macro, and Mechanisms." In *The Oxford Handbook of Philosophy of the Social Sciences*, edited by Harold Kincaid, 21–45. Oxford: Oxford University Press.
—2013. "Causal and Constitutive Explanation Compared." *Erkenntnis* 78: 277–97.

—2014. "Rethinking Micro-Macro Relations." In *Rethinking the Individualism-Holism Debate: Essays in the Philosophy of Social Science*, edited by Julie Zahle and Finn Collin, 117–35. Cham: Springer.

Zacks, Jeffrey M., Nicole K. Speer, Khena M. Swallow, Todd S. Braver, and Jeremy R. Reynolds. 2007. "Event Perception: A Mind-Brain Perspective." *Psychological Bulletin* 133(2): 273–93.

Zacks, Jeffrey M., and Barbara Tversky. 2001. "Event Structure in Perception and Conception." *Psychological Bulletin* 127: 3–21.

2

Between a Rock and a Hard Place: Analysing the Reception of and Debate over the Building Block Approach

Göran Larsson
University of Gothenburg

By Way of Introduction

If I have understood Taves and Asprem correctly, it should be the duty of all serious scholars of religion to pay attention to research based on so-called "social construction" or "naturalist" theories. As a result, Taves' and Asprem's thought-provoking perspective involves combining these two ideal-type approaches into a unified system: "Our goal, in other words, is not to subsume or subordinate the humanities to the natural and social sciences, but to connect them in a spirit of consilience" (Asprem and Taves 2018a: 134).

Although I believe that this is an admirable and vital ambition, it has not convinced all camps in the study of religion, as this short text will try to demonstrate. By assessing a number of reviews and debates concerning the author's Building Block Approach (henceforth BBA), I aim to show Taves' and Asprem's readers how their theoretical and methodological suggestions have been received by the academic community.

While the BBA has received a lot of attention, I will primarily analyse reviews and critical texts written by scholars who advocate "constructionist" or "naturalistic" theories and methods.[1] Although I will highlight the advantages, problems and challenges that different reviewers have associated with the BBA, I will not assess the quality of the criticisms that Taves and Asprem have received, nor will I judge whether the descriptions

---

1. According to ATLA, a database of bibliographical information on religious studies, Taves' book has been reviewed several times in leading journals and was the focus of a special issue of *Religion* (2010) 40(4). See also Stausberg (2010) for an introduction, description and analysis of some of the debates that Taves has raised.

and suggestion that the reviewers make of the "other" camp, that of the "constructionist" or "naturalistic" theories, are either nuanced or fair.

As the originator of the BBA, Taves has published more extensively than Asprem and has received more attention. My discussion will therefore be devoted primarily to reviews of her book *Religious Experience Reconsidered: A Building Block Approach to the Study of Religion and Other Special Things* (2011). However, another work, *Method Today: Redescribing Approaches to the Study of Religion*, edited by Brad Stoddard in 2018, also provides information on how Taves' and Asprem's suggestions have been received. To demonstrate the problems involved in combining "constructionist" and "naturalist" theories and methods, I will highlight especially two reviews of *Religious Experience Reconsidered*, one by Russell T. McCutcheon, who is seen as a representative of the social construction approach, the other by Luther H. Martin and Donald Wiebe, who are seen as representatives of both the naturalistic and cognitive approaches to the study of religion.

A Rock and the Hard Place

Before I turn to the reviews and debates, it is first necessary to say something briefly about what the BBA entails. This is a complex question, and it is actually quite hard to find a simple summary of what Taves and Asprem mean by the BBA. One suggestion, however, is given in the following quote:

> The building block approach (hereafter BBA) is a method for analysing – and explaining – complex cultural phenomena in terms of the constituent parts that interact to produce them. By *constituent parts*, we refer to all the cognitive, psychological, and biological processes that guide human interaction with the environment (natural, built, and social) from perception and affect to memorization, categorization, and strategizing. While many scholars of religion are likely to agree that culture cannot emerge apart from the biological organisms that create it, it is often far less clear how one can relate the cultural to the biological in a meaningful way. This has created a methodological chasm between the "holistic" appreciation of cultural complexity and the "reductionist" explanatory efforts of the natural sciences that we are attempting to bridge with our building block approach. In particular, the approach is designed to solve two related questions: (1) what terminology should we use when analysing and explaining cultural phenomena (such as "religions"), and (2) how can we achieve consilience between natural, behavioural, and humanistic sciences? Or, to put it in epistomological terms, how can we bridge the divide between naturalists and constructionists? (Taves and Asprem, this volume, p. 4)

With this summary of the BBA before us, it is now possible to turn to the reviews and debates. For example, while it is likely that Luther Martin and Donald Wiebe, two scholars who could be considered advocates of naturalistic explanations, find several aspects of the BBA promising, they are very pessimistic about Taves' argument of the necessity of bridging the divide that exists between social construction and naturalistic explanations. But also her use of scholars associated with the field of esotericism such as Wouter J. Hanegraff (b. 1961) and Kocku von Stuckrad (b. 1966), clearly awakens genuine suspicions among these two scholars. They write: "Unlike the aspirations and methods of the natural sciences which are 'scientific,' Taves understands those of religious studies to be 'mixed' and, like many in the field of religious studies, she affirms the appropriateness of this polymethodological mishmash" (Martin and Wiebe 2012: 620).

On the basis of this quote, they assert that Taves is open to the possibility that religious studies should remain a cornerstone of the North American Liberal Arts tradition, that is, that the aim of academic studies should be to educate and foster caring and moral citizens (Martin and Wiebe 2012: 618). If we are to believe Martin and Wiebe (p. 620), Taves seems to think that academic studies should strive for the "moral and spiritual formation of students", instead of only seeking objective truths, that is, knowledge for the sake of knowledge and nothing else (for an outline of their views on religious studies, see Wiebe 1988; see also D'Andrade 1995 for a description of the tension between what he sees as objective and moral models of doing research). Taves' apparently lax attitude towards science – at least according to these two reviewers – leaves room for spiritual emotions and experiences, which disturbs Martin and Wiebe, who would like to close off all other options apart from the empirical study of religions. For them, the only aim that scholars of religion should embrace is to seek objective truths and explain religion as a human phenomenon. For them, also, it is a contradiction in terms to speak about truths in the plural and, in agreement with Roy D'Andrade, they find it important to make a distinction between objective and subjective descriptions. In D'Andrade's own words, an "objective description tells about the thing described, not about the agent doing the description, while a subjective description tells how the agent doing the description *reacts* to the object" (D'Andrade 1995: 399). Echoing D'Andrade's conclusions, it should come as no surprise that Martin and Wiebe have problems with the following statement found in the opening section of Taves' book:

> My [i.e. Taves'] own view is that the cultivation of some forms of experience that we might want to deem religious or spiritual can enhance our well-being and our ability to function in the world, individually and collectively. Identifying those forms, however, is not the purpose of this book. (Taves 2011: xiv)

While Martin and Wiebe think that Taves is willing to accept a "polymethodological mishmash" when she gives space to "well-being, and our ability to function in the world", Russell T. McCutcheon, an American scholar who stresses the importance of language, social constructions and power in the study of religions, provides a completely different reading of *Religious Experience Reconsidered*. His main concern is Taves' interest in naturalistic explanations. He writes:

> What therefore troubles me about the attempt to find religious experiences in the mind/brain or religion in the genes is the manner in which, despite the sophistication that informs its use, a culturally and historically local nomenclature (i.e., this is religion, that is not religion) is being dehistoricized and thus normalized by being medicalized and thus naturalized. This troubles me because we all know – or at least I thought we did – of the critiques of the category religion as it was once used (I think here of critiques of the notion of sui generis religion). We all know that none of its possible Latin precursors likely meant what we mean by religion today (or at least as we have commonly defined it for the past few hundred years). We also all know that both this and the previous sentence's "we" are something that always need attention, for they signify a rather precise group, originating in that part of the world commonly known as Europe, whose members eventually perfected the use of the marker "religion" to name a seemingly distinct domain of diverse (though not necessarily inherently related) items of human activity and production. (McCutcheon 2010: 1185)

According to McCutcheon, instead of embracing the hyperbolic claim that it is possible to explain something called religion in a naturalistic way, as proposed by many scholars associated with the cognitive study of religion (at least according to McCutcheon's reading) the serious researcher should instead pay attention to questions of classification, language and social formations. How can we explain religion if we do not pay critical attention to how we define it? To replace "religious experiences" with "special experiences", to use Taves' phraseology, does not solve the problem for McCutcheon. He believes that "we still end up finding people the world over who see 'religion-like' things as like" (McCutcheon 2010: 1186). This conclusion implies that our understanding of the world is restricted by the confines of language (i.e. it is our definitions and classifications that determine how we see the world), and as a consequence we have learned to see the world in specific ways and have thus acquired explicit tastes and a habitus.

This epistemological problem, namely that the social formation of the world is entwined with and closely related to language and culture, is seldom addressed critically by those who embrace naturalistic explanations, at least if we believe McCutcheon's outline and conclusion:

> For some time I [McCutcheon] have been perplexed by how willing many serious scholars are to adopt untheorized folk taxon, as if a classification used by a group we *happen* to study somehow corresponds to an actual aspect of reality that *needs* to be studied. (McCutcheon 2010: 1186–87)

To McCutcheon "religion", at least as we (i.e. at Western universities) know it, is not a cross-cultural or universal reality, as many scholars who advocate naturalistic explanations seem to believe. McCutcheon maintains that different people both past and present have used different "complex taxonomic systems that they use to signify, classify, and thereby sort their world, yet scholars do not necessarily develop a scientific study of each of these taxons, thereby conceiving of them as universal properties of the human" (p. 1187). At least according to McCutcheon, therefore, the ambition to explain "religion" is an impossible and naïve enterprise demonstrating merely that those who advocate naturalistic explanations do not understand the implications of their theoretical claims. Since there is no unified or uncontested definition of what should be counted as religion or seen as religious, it is naïve to think that a universal scientific theory can be developed to explain religion (e.g. Boyer 2001). It can therefore be argued that many followers of the cognitive study of religion use a vague folk taxon at best, a procedure with which they try and develop a theory of something that is not easily agreed upon. To demonstrate his point, McCutcheon uses Harvey Whitehouse's *Modes of Religiosity: A Cognitive Theory of Religious Transmission* (2004). After Whitehouse has given examples and argued that it is not easy to pin down what is meant by religion, especially if you are interested in research that includes materials from different times and places, he still ends up with the conclusion that it is necessary to search for "scientific theories of religion" (p. 2). This is a lamentable conclusion to McCutcheon, who asks "a theory of what?" (2010: 1187). Instead of looking at "religion" as a discursive practice (cf. Taira 2013; von Stuckrad 2013), the naturalistic approach is simply a new form of "sui generis religion re-entering our field, doing it this time through a new, biological back door" (McCutcheon 2010: 1191).

Combining the Un-combinable, or Simply a Matter of Taste?

Without siding with any of the readings of Taves' book presented in the former section, it is interesting to ask ourselves why these reviewers are so divided when it comes to social construction and naturalistic explanations, and in addition why they find it so provocative when a scholar tries to mix and blend these two ideal-type approaches? For those of us who have few or no problems with this ambition, it is difficult to conceive how much conflict and discord Taves' suggestions have stirred up among our colleagues in the field of religious studies (see, e.g., Curtis 2010; Simmons 2012). A conclusion suggested by Curtis is that Taves' *Religious Experience Reconsidered* is "a sign of a global apocalypse that will kill us all", as it advances a "normative secularism" and makes possible reductionistic explanations of religion (Curtis 2010: 292).

Another sensitive issue is that Taves is not interested in defining what should be counted as "religion" or "religious", a problem that has tormented and divided the study of religion from the very start (e.g. Dubuisson 2015). However, since this is a problem with no solution in sight, Taves argues convincingly that it is more fruitful to open up the field and discuss things that have been deemed religious or that humans tend to set aside as "special". She writes:

> ... I [Taves] argue that the use of "religious" or any other first-order term, such as "numinous", "sacred," "mystical," "spiritual," or "magical" as a means of specifying an object of study is both limiting and confusing and suggest instead that investigation of the broader, more generic category of "special things" and "things set apart" may be more helpful for the purposes of research. Building on Durkheim, I distinguish between things that people view as special or that they set apart, on the one hand, and the systems of beliefs and practices that some people associate with some special things, on the other. The former involves a simple ascription (of specialness), and the latter a composite ascription (of efficacy to practices associated with special things) characteristic of what we think of as *religions* or *spiritualities*. (Taves 2011: 17)

However, this procedure and solution to the old problem of how to define religion does not satisfy all readers, and Taves has therefore been accused of using an implicit definition rooted in the assumption that, "when we see something religious, we know that it is religious". Although her definition is broad and inclusive, it is unfair to argue that she is unaware of this problem. On the contrary, by studying how, when and why something is deemed religious or is set apart as special, the scholar – at least if we accept Taves' and Asprem's propositions – is given an important key to studying what is at issue when something is "made into something religious or special". This process is called "reverse engineering" by Taves and Asprem (a concrete example of how to apply this procedure is found in Asprem 2016). As stated in the introduction by Taves and Asprem to this volume:

> ... reverse engineering entails a series of steps designed to take apart a complex system and analyse its constituent parts in order to (1) find out how it works and (2) trace how the parts (events, actions, and representations) have been assembled and labelled in specific formations. (p. 9)

According to Asprem and Taves, this method (i.e. the reverse engineering) will help the scholar to locate, analyse and disentangle "complex cultural concepts" (CCC), that is, "abstract nouns with unstable, overlapping meanings that vary within and across social formations" (p. 9), like "religious", "spiritual", "sacred", "occult", and so on. By using this procedure, it is possible to "redescribe specific phenomena enlisted under CCCs as something (a basic concept) that is appraised in more specific cultural terms" (Taves and Asprem, p. 6). As compared to CCC, the basic concepts (BC) "translate relatively easily across formations and levels because they refer to broadly shared aspects of human experience, rooted in embodied interactions with the environment and evolved mental architecture shared by the entire species" (p. 9). Instead of talking about a specific "ritual" or "belief" – two complex cultural concepts – we should talk about actions, events, representations, schemata or models, for example, concepts that are "grounded in evolved mental architectures and embodied interactions with the environment". Also, using this procedure, our concepts become more stable and recognizable across cultures, time and space (Asprem 2016: 160–61). This methodological approach will make it possible for the researcher to break down the study object (i.e. the thing, event, phenomena, behaviour, etc. that we would like to know something about) into lower-level building blocks that can be placed in a chain of events which, pieced together, constitutes the phenomena we would like to study. In making this suggestion, Taves and Asprem are influenced by philosophers who adhere to the so-called "new mechanical philosophy", which studies the "parts" that "produce the phenomenon" (Glennan 2016). This approach is summarized in the following quote: "What makes a model a mechanical model is that it represents how the entities act and interact in order to be responsible for the mechanism's phenomena" (Glennan 2016: 804).

However, many scholars of religion have expressed serious doubts about this possibility – some of its most outspoken critics have been included in my discussion – or pointed out that Asprem's and Taves' suggestions are not that new (e.g. Nordin, this volume, pp. 55–66). Others have been terrified by the prospect that the broad definitions and methods they have proposed will make all departments of religious studies obsolete and unnecessary. A more positive reading of Taves and Asprem is that their (broad) definition will open up doors for researchers who have studied phenomena that are deemed religious and that this could lead to new and more innovative collaborations. This may well encourage the development of novel research areas and possibly also new university bodies seeking consilience, with fresh ways of organizing the university, new departments, areas of expertise, and more.

A third criticism is that Taves and Asprem also leave "the political" out of their theoretical suggestions. This objection seems to suggest that they do not care about values or claims made by the subjects being studied or that scholars have responsibilities to their objects (Dew 2018). With their supposedly objective approach, according to their critics, Taves and Asprem run the risk of forgetting that they also have biases when it comes to classifications and are just as likely to be under the influence of folk categories. However, if we hark back to the words of Martin and Wiebe, the aim of research should only be to discover the Truth (with a capital T). Thus, it is unnecessary, even wrong, to ponder long over the possible outcomes of one's studies. This opinion is expressed by Wiebe, who writes:

> ... the academic study of religion must be undertaken for academic – that is, purely intellectual/scientific – reasons and not as instrumental in the achievement of religious, cultural, political or other ends. This means, quite simply, that the academic/scientific study of religion must aim only at understanding religion where "understanding" is mediated through an intersubjectively testable set of statements about religious phenomena and religious traditions. As with any other scientific enterprise, therefore, the academic study of religion aims at public knowledge of public facts ... (Wiebe 1988: 407)

However, for scholars who, for example, would like to make a moral contribution to society or a religious community, this is at best a bizarre suggestion. For many researchers who apply so-called critical theory, feminist, post-colonial and theological theories, the primary aim of research is often (if not always) to make a positive contribution to society, at least according to their understandings. Thus, as they argue, it is necessary to contribute and make a change for the better. This emphasis resembles the shift that Roy D'Andrade wrote about critically in respect of social anthropology and what he sees as its weak position within the sciences today (cf. Boyer 2011). According to D'Andrade, instead of conducting empirical research in the form of research programs that are possible to test intersubjectively and are replicable, many researchers in the social and humanistic sciences who conduct so-called engaged research have shifted the focus to providing moralistic answers to scientific questions. Instead of describing the object with the aim of learning something about it, the ambition is to say something about how the "agent doing the description *reacts* to the object" (D'Andrade 1995: 399). Thus, the primary ambition is to uncover so-called power regimes and hegemonies in order to liberate the object that one studies: in other words, this is a deliberative enterprise. This post-modern shift has led to relativism and alternative facts, according to D'Andrade (1995; cf. Boyer 2011).

A Matter of the Philosophy of Science and a Way Forward

However, D'Andrade's criticism does not involve denying that all scholars are likely to approach their data, whether texts, human behaviour, genes, or owls, and so on, with some preconceived ideas about their research objects. In other words, we all have a theory about the world and the objects we study. While inference from induction – that is, that we start from our observations of the facts – can be an ideal, it is more realistic to argue that we start with some kind of inference from deduction (i.e. with a theory about the world). Using the following anecdote, the philosopher of science Karl Popper (1902–1994) shows convincingly that deductive reasoning is the normal way of understanding the world.

> 25 years ago, I tried [Karl R. Popper] to illustrate the same points for a group of physics students in Vienna by starting the lecture with the following task: "Get pen and paper; Observe carefully and write down what you have observed!" Of course, they asked what I wanted them to observe. Of course, the task "Observe!" Is absurd ... An observation is always selective. It requires a selection of objects, a definite task, an interest, a perspective, a problem. (Quoted in Gilje and Grimen 1993: 89, my translation)

Even if I agree with Popper – a statement that also resonates with how most researchers understand the world and how so-called critical realists understands science – it is still possible to differentiate between opinions, facts and different scientific modes (cf. Boyer 2011; D'Andrade 1995). Let me be very clear: I believe that we should expect academic research to consist of something other than opinion-forming, everyday conversations, journalism, speculation or popular opinion. For example, it is reasonable to argue that all researchers should be aware of their own preconceived understandings of what they are studying and should have enough training to be able to bracket out their own opinions about the topic that they want to study (cf., for example, Asprem and Taves 2018b: 199). The researcher should, for example, ask open questions and be prepared to have his or her findings tested by the research community. One's study should be based on what Pascal Boyer calls either the science or the erudition mode. While the first mode strives for naturalistic explanations that are based on empirical observations, the other mode is focused more on describing and systematizing the empirical data. As Boyer points out, however, most researchers and academic disciplines include both modes, which in any case are of equal importance for our knowledge (Boyer 2011: 7–10).

If we agree with Boyer's description of the science and erudition modes, I wonder how we should understand the criticisms that have been directed at Taves and Asprem for emphasizing the necessity of explanation in the study of religions and for promoting the BBA? As I have already implied, one possible suggestion is that scholars of religious studies have paid too little attention to debates and developments within the broad field of the philosophy of science, especially the so-called "new mechanical philosophy" that underpins Asprem's and Taves' works. For example, to do justice to the BBA, as suggested by Taves and Asprem, one must ask whether it is possible to combine an outlook that views the world primarily as a social construction (i.e. how we *perceive* the world in our heads) with a scientific understanding which tries to uncover natural and causal laws (i.e. how the world *is* empirically) that are universal rather than specific

2 Between a Rock and a Hard Place

or unique to a distinct period or context. In other words, is it possible to break down complex cultural nouns – like "religion" or "sacred" – and redescribe them as so-called basic concepts or building blocks? A basic requirement is that we understand the underpinnings of our theoretical outlooks and that we know what kind of scientific modes we are operating with (cf. Boyer 2011). Are we working in a mode that looks for natural explanations, causality and covering laws (i.e. the scientific mode, which seeks explanations), or are we mainly devoted to descriptions and taxonomies or typologies (i.e. the erudite mode, which tries to describe and systematize our findings without looking for explanations)? To be aware of these differences does not mean saying that one mode is better than the other – on the contrary – and the two modes described above are generally combined by most researchers and sciences. Which mode one applies often depends on one's personal taste and skills, but the focus can also be related to the kinds of questions and scientific problems we are trying to solve at the moment. No matter which mode we choose to follow, or whether we combine the scientific and erudite modes (as is the case for Taves' and Asprem's BBA), I think most researchers would agree that a serious problem arises when they decide to leave the two scientific paths described by Boyer and become engaged in something that can merely be described as uninformed opinion-making and moral judgments. Despite all their disagreements and interests, I think McCutcheon, Wiebe, Martin, Taves, Asprem and all the other reviewers I have covered in this text would agree that this is the overarching danger for all scientific work and for the university at large.

Thus, if we can agree that this is the problem, leave behind the "polemical boundary-skirmishes in the study of religion" (Asprem 2016: 179) and try to bridge the divide that unfortunately often seems to exists between the scientific and erudite modes, scholars of religions must, I argue, pay more attention to theoretical and methodological questions in order to undertake more solid studies that seek consilience. However, in order to seek consilience, it is also vital to approach and test those methods and theories that we are less likely to accept (we all suffer from confirmation bias, no matter whether our taste is for social constructionist theories or naturalistic explanations). As a first step, we should start by critically discussing the scientific and philosophical ideas that underpin those of the theories under discussion we trust, but we should also pay great if not greater attention to theories and methods we find doubtful for some reason or another. Vital questions to be raised are how the major theories used in religious studies relate to classical debates on topics like realism versus idealism, what is entailed by explanation, does a theory seek general or specific explanations, what do empirical data and causality entail, how should we study the distribution of power and gender structures in the society in past and present empirically, and so on? While it is easy to come up with a new theory, the real scientific task is to test the theory.

While social constructionist theories try to interpret specific episodes or texts, often with the help of a so-called critical hermeneutics, a discourse analysis (e.g. von Stuckrad 2013) or a genealogical approach (Asad 1993), scholars who are influenced by a reductionistic and naturalistic approach seek explanations that are valid for the whole human race, regardless of time, place or culture (e.g. Boyer 2001). This distinction can also be framed as a tension between a focus on the particular and the search for the universal. Jesper Sørensen describes this tension when he writes:

> These two problems reveal a tension between a nomothetic approach that is inherently universalistic and synchronic in its attempt to explain general features of the human mind and an ideographic approach seeking to interpret the diachronic unfolding of particular and historically embedded discursive universes. (Sørensen 2017: 119–20)

Whereas Asprem and Taves think that it is it possible to combine both approaches, which I too believe is feasible, one needs to understand that both the premise and the possible outcomes of socially constructionist and naturalistic theories are different and that our choices will have an impact on how we see the world (i.e. our epistemology). To avoid unnecessary confusion, it is essential to pay close attention to possible differences that will have an impact on the final outcome. Both theoretical approaches can be used provided we are aware that they will provide different tools for analysing and explaining the world. Again, it is our research questions and interests that drive us to adopt different theoretical and methodological positions. One possible hypothesis is that a social constructivist approach is more suitable if we are interested in questions related to power and authority, that is, interpretations of historical data; but if we are more interested in why humans behave and respond to the world in certain ways, it is most likely better to pay attention to naturalistic explanations. While it is possible to argue that constructionist theories and methods and naturalistic explanations provide answers on different levels, it remains necessary to seek consilience and to combine different methods and theories to solve complex scientific problems. One way of doing this is to adopt the BBA suggested by Taves and Asprem.

Conclusion

By accepting that various theoretical and methodological tools can be used for diverse tasks (at least on different aggregated levels or for specific parts in the reverse-engineering process or in the chain that constitutes the building blocks that we are interested in analysing), it is possible – at least in my understanding – to cross the troubled waters that divide academia when it comes to questions of social construction and naturalism. If I understand the processes that Asprem and Taves call "reverse engineering" correctly, this approach can help us break down complex cultural concepts. Having taken this step – which is very much in line with what social constructionists normally do – it becomes possible to "redescribe specific phenomena enlisted under CCCs as something (a basic concept)" and thus change the perspective or scale of the analysis, turn to explanations (i.e. the naturalistic side of research) and ask why humans have capacities that can be used to express or understand the specific phenomena under study. By taking all these necessary steps, it becomes possible to lay out the blocks that make up the phenomena we are studying (both from the social constructionist and the naturalistic points of view), which gives us all the vital parts that make up the machine (if I may use this metaphor) according to the so-called "mechanical philosophy". In Asprem's and Taves' words, this is the building block approach.

About the Author

Göran Larsson is a Professor in the study of religions at the University of Gothenburg. His main research focus is Islam and Muslims in Europe both past and present, but he also has a general interest in theoretical and methodological questions concerning the study of humans, especially with regard to religion. Besides these topics, Larsson has also conducted research on global conflicts and how they impact on Swedish society. He has published several books, chapters and articles with international publishing houses, for example, Brill, Routledge, Springer, and Ashgate.

References

Asad, Talal. 1993. *Genealogies of Religion: Discipline and Reasons of Power in Christianity and Islam.* Baltimore: The Johns Hopkins University Press.
Asprem, Egil. 2016. "Reverse-Engineering 'Esotericism': How to Prepare a Complex Cultural Concept for the Cognitive Science of Religion." *Religion* 46(2): 158–85.
Asprem, Egil, and Ann Taves. 2018a. "Explanation and the Study of Religion." In Stoddard 2018: 133–57.
—2018b. "To Our Critics." In Stoddard 2018: 192–201.
Boyer, Pascal. 2001. *Religion Explained: The Human Instincts that Fashion Gods, Spirits and Ancestors.* London: Vintage Books.
—2011. "From Studious Irrelevancy to Consilient Knowledge: Modes of Scholarship and Cultural Anthropology." In *Creating Consilience: Evolution, Cognitive Science, and the Humanities,* edited by Edward Slingerland and Mark Collard, 113–29. Oxford: Oxford University Press.

Curtis, Finbarr. 2010. "Ann Taves's Religious Experience Reconsidered is a Sign of Global Apocalypse That Will Kill Us All." *Religion* 40(4): 288–92.
D'Andrade, Roy. 1995. "Moral Models in Anthropology." *Current Anthropology* 36(3): 399–408.
Dew, Spencer. 2018. "'Constitutional God-Given Rights': Explaining Religion and Politics in the Malheur Occupation." In Stoddard 2018: 158–67.
Dubuisson, Daniel. 2015. "Definitions of Religion." In *Vocabulary for the Study of Religion*, edited by Robert A. Segal and Kocku von Stuckrad, Vol. 1, 392–96. Leiden and Boston: Brill.
Gilje, Nils, and Harald Grimen. 1992. *Samhällsvetenskapens förutsättningar* (Swedish translation Sten Andersson). Göteborg: Daidalos.
Glennan, Stuart. 2016. "Mechanisms and Mechanical Philosophy." In *The Oxford Handbook of Philosophy of Science*, edited by Paul Humphreys, 796–816. Oxford: Oxford University Press.
Martin, H. Luther, and Donald Wiebe. 2012. "When Pessimism is Realism: A Rejoinder to our Colleagues." *Journal of the American Academy of Religion* 80(3): 618–22.
McCutcheon, Russell T. 2010. "Will your Cognitive Anchor Hold in the Storms of Culture?" *Journal of the American Academy of Religion* 78(4): 1182–.93.
Simmons, Merinda K. 2012. "The Experiential Elephant and the Pursuit of Interdisciplinarity." *Bulletin for the Study of Religion* 41(3): 2–6.
Sørensen, Jesper. 2017. "Western Esotericism and Cognitive Science of Religion." *Aries: Journal for the Study of Western Esotericism* 17(1): 119–35.
Stausberg, Michael. 2010. "From 1799 to 2009: *Religious Experience Reconsidered* - Background, Argument, Responses." *Religion* 40(4): 279–85.
Stoddard, Brad, ed. 2018. *Method Today: Redescribing Approaches to the Study of Religion*. Sheffield: Equinox.
Taira, Temu. 2013. "Making Space for Discursive Study in Religious Studies." *Religion* 43(1): 26–45.
Taves, Ann. 2011 [2009]. *Religious Experience Reconsidered: A Building Block Approach to the Study of Religion and Other Special Things*. Princeton, NJ: Princeton University Press.
von Stuckrad, Kocku. 2013. "Discursive Study of Religion: Approaches, Definitions, Implications." *Method and Theory in the Study of Religion* 25: 5–25.
Whitehouse, Harvey. 2004. *Modes of Religiosity: A Cognitive Theory of Religious Transmission*. Walnut Creek: Altamira Press.
Wiebe, Donald. 1988. "'Why the Academic Study of Religion?' Motive and Method in the Study of Religion." *Religious Studies* 24: 403–13.

3

Fantastic Stories, Emotions, and Ancient Religions: Open Questions and Ideas in Conversation with the Building Block and Worldviews Approach

Laura Feldt
University of Southern Denmark

In response to Ann Taves' and Egil Asprem's approach to religious experience, the building blocks and worldviews approach (Taves 2011; Taves and Asprem 2017, 2018), and the general attempt to achieve more consilience between the natural and the humanistic and social sciences that Taves' and Asprem's work entails, I would like to raise and discuss three related issues and some open questions. The issues and questions spring from work of my own on ancient religions, mediality (Feldt and Høgel 2018), and the emotions (Feldt forthcoming; Feldt 2017) that has revolved around similar kinds of material: religious stories of fantastic, horrific, monstrous, and extraordinary events and experiences.

However, I would like to start with another point, one that intersects with the three issues. The interests and agenda that lie behind the BBA are in some ways similar to my own. I also use the basic standpoint of a critical, moderate constructivism on naturalistic (Taves and Asprem, this volume, pp. 5-25) and realist grounds in my own work (Feldt 2016c, drawing on the work of Jensen 2003 and Schaffalitzky de Muckadell 2014), and I generally applaud the quest for more consilience between the sciences. Yet, as a scholar specializing in ancient religions as well as religion and contemporary popular culture, and having been invited to comment on Taves' and Asprem's work in that capacity, not as a specialist of the cognitive science of religion or the BBA, I find myself asking my first questions "from the other end", as it were. In other words, I find other kinds of questions and approaches more pressing when researching both ancient religions and contemporary popular culture than those favoured by the BBA. However, some fascinating areas of common concern and inquiry can be found. As my title indicates, this chapter will thus neither test the theory or use it; nor will this chapter reject the theory. The chapter offers a discussion of some open questions, as well as some feedback and ideas in relation to the BBA, from the viewpoint of a historian of religion, not a cognitive scientist of religion. These questions and ideas, however, are intended to raise issues of broader relevance and common concern that are important if we want a dialogue, in the general study of religions, between specialists of the cognitive science of religion and other historians of religion.

Asking Questions from the Other End: The Role of Media and Materiality

My first response to the BBA is to notice the delegation of media and materiality issues to the background. The BBA seems to start from a great interest in what happens *behind* narratives and experiences (Taves and Asprem, this volume, p. 117; 2017), in tracing the generation of experience backwards to original experience-events (Taves and Asprem 2017), or at least in reverse-engineering in order to identify constituent parts and how they are assembled and labelled (Taves and Asprem, this volume, p. 9). Contrariwise, my work usually starts from an interest in what happens *in front of* narratives (or sources in a broader sense), in paying attention to the role of media and materiality in experience and narrative formation, and to place the performativity of narratives and social frames and contexts in the foreground. Firstly, this is related to how in some of the religious materials I work on, there might not be any experience *behind* a narrative of an experience (this is, for example, true for many stories from the Hebrew Bible, see Feldt 2011a, 2011b), and even if there were, it cannot be located or accessed by historians of religion, while there are certainly experiences in *front* of them that can be analysed – experiences generated by the stories. In many ways, I find it more pressing for historians of religion seeking to understand the broader phenomenon of "religion" – and the various expressions, practices, phenomena, representations, and experiences that this concept involves – to look at how, for example, experiences can be stimulated, trained, and practised via media and forms of materiality.

We can of course call the different aspects that a concept of religion involves – rituals, myths, material culture, experience, and so on – "building blocks" in a very general sense. Yet that terminology could entail too little emphasis on emergent meanings and context (cf. Ricoeur 1965, 1975; Jensen 2003, 2009); features of key importance for understanding lived religion/s as sociocultural phenomena.[1] But to be sure, in a very broad

---

1. Emergent meaning also receives some attention in the cognitive science of religion, e.g., in Fauconnier and Turner (2002).

sense, the idea of "religion" as composite and made up of other phenomena, aspects, practices, and so on is very useful in a general, but also somewhat trivial, sense, and it is already present in many concepts of religion (cf. Geertz 1999; Gilhus and Mikaelsson 2001; Sutcliffe and Gilhus 2013; see also Segal 2006 for a snappy discussion). For that reason, let me say that when I refer to the BBA in this piece, I mean Ann Taves' and Egil Asprem's current exposition of it (this volume, p. 5). In addition, as a historian of religion, not a cognition specialist, one will also often be more interested in the later re-narrations, social contexts, and emergent meanings that work towards keeping religions as social formations in the existential game, as it were, rather than in reverse-engineering building blocks. Especially when we take into account how religions may be built on or make use of self-reflectively fictitious stories too, not only in fiction-based religions in the contemporary era, but also in the long history of religions; narratives for which original events (that can then be appraised unconsciously and labelled consciously) cannot be located.[2] Nevertheless, that certainly does not mean that Taves' and Asprem's research agenda could not also in principle be made relevant for these kinds of interests.[3]

Secondly, another factor behind my interest in asking other kinds of questions is related to subjectivity formation – for which analyses of experience, memory, and emotion formation are also relevant. I work based on the view that subjectivity formation is only possible within social frames (Butler 2005), and that any narrative of an event, also a first-person narrative, is always-already shaped by existing cultural frames (Feldt 2011b), a viewpoint Taves and Asprem seem to agree to, at least to a certain extent (Taves and Asprem, this volume, pp. 5–25), even though it makes a simple reverse-engineering very complicated.

This is just to indicate, initially, how my work usually proceeds from turning Taves' and Asprem's initial foreground into background, and asking questions from the other end, as it were. Whichever end we might start from, I agree that we as historians of religions need to work on naturalist and realist grounds and to aim for as much consilience as possible. But we also need to pay attention to emergent meanings, social context, as well as media and materiality, especially in order to loosen

---

2. As I show in my analysis of the Exodus narrative, the question of ficticity looms large within that story itself, and this is the object of reflection within the story (Feldt 2011a). For other religious formations, fiction can form the core narrative (see Davidsen 2016; Petersen 2016; Feldt 2016b). It is interesting to note that the scholars seeking naturalistic explanations of the original events and the religionists seeking supernatural explanations of the same posited original events agree on the importance of *original experience events*. I think this underestimates the power of fabrications, fantasy, and mediality and the human imagination.

3. A kind of forward-engineering, perhaps, to use Taves/Asprem terminology.

up our discipline's long-standing bias towards beliefs and inner experiences. So, we also need to investigate how narratives and other religious material media stimulate and affect the senses, bodies, and emotions of the audiences, that is, how religious narratives, forms of materiality, paraphernalia, spaces, sounds, and buildings (etc.) help *stimulate, train and form experience.*

Furthermore, in addition to the "interior" special things that seemed to be at the centre of Taves' book (2011, originally published in 2009), that is, stories of unusual events related to the interior person or human bodies, I find it important that we also analyse experiences stimulated by, for instance, narratives of the fantastic, and unusual and horrific marvels located in the exterior world. Stories of "exterior" special things, that is, marvels, unusual events, weird and eerie happenings, and so on, that are believed to happen in the exterior world, like for example bushes that burn without being consumed, bleeding hosts, or monsters attacking castles, and similar things, are very common in the long history of religions (Feldt 2011a); and these stories that scare, horrify, titillate or cause hesitation, surprise, wonder, and so on – seem to me to be quite related to the kinds of experience stories that Ann Taves has been interested in – while they do not invariably relate back to any original experiences that are then processed and appraised. Such stories are often more clearly made-up. The narratives of such fantastic events, actions, material things, beings, and spaces can be studied in terms of their aesthetic (Gr., *aesthesis*, cf. Feldt 2017) mediality – how they affect experiences, emotions, and sensory responses. Let me elaborate.

Fantastic stories

In my book *The Fantastic in Religious Narrative from Exodus to Elisha* (2012a) I was interested in analysing the role and functions of fantastic narratives in religions – stories of unusual occurrences, marvels, miracles, and other special happenings – and a good way of doing that seemed to me to be to compare religious narratives with the literary genres of the fantastic and fantasy – a move that can, in retrospect, be compared with Ann Taves' move to compare religious special things with other special things (Taves 2011). I argued that theoretical perspectives drawn from theories of fantasy and the fantastic could provide more adequate ways of dealing with such types of religious narrative than the traditional category of "miracle narrative" and also bring new perspectives to myth theory (Feldt 2011a, 2012a). For example, by using a comparative fantasy-theoretical perspective, we can analyse miracle narratives, narratives about magic, marvels, ghosts, monsters, fantastic regions, metamorphoses, visions, elves, magicians and others, while avoiding the many problems related to the miracle versus magic terminology that is entrenched in emic discursive power struggles. All such fantastic elements can be theorized and analysed together in terms of how they are narratively embedded, their literary form and performativity – that is, how they stimulate reactions, experiences, and emotions in the audiences. Image-intensive, titillating religious narratives about fantastic beings, events, actions, or places – such as "Woman Gave Birth to Egg", "Statue Drank Real Milk", or "People Crossed Sea on Dry Ground" (cf. Feldt 2011a) – are stories that emphasize the marvel of the religious "manifestation" or "experience", its ambiguity and uncertainty, that are emotionally and cognitively exciting, that include manifestations that horrify and scare, as well as those that are seen as benign and comforting. In this perspective, the focus is thus not on any events behind the stories, but instead on how the stories *stimulate* experience in their audiences. I found that these narrative contexts, in which counterintuitive representations were embedded, were crucial for understanding the experiential and emotional impact of the narratives on recipients, how the narratives represent and negotiate the status of the "phantasms" and which types of stimuli are cultivated by different types of stories (see here also Feldt 2017; Feldt forthcoming). This means that my interest here lies more with the cumulative impact of the stories, the social context, and the emergent meanings and effects, rather than with reverse-engineering back to original experiences, not only because those experiences are either inaccessible to historians or because the stories are made-up, but also because cumulative impact, social context, and emergent meanings and effects should also be within our purview. For that reason, I suggest that the BBA adds some attention to the experiential impact of made-up stories.

This work of comparing fantasy narratives with religious narratives, and analysing fantastic stories in Hebrew Bible and ancient Mesopotamian religions, led me to the argument that religious narratives can be seen as a subset of a broader set of fantastic and fantasy narratives, with special pragmatic determinants – or, in other words, that religious narratives are fantasy narratives that become "religious" via ascription and specific forms of use (see also Feldt 2006, 2012a). More recently I have, in dialogue with Davidsen (2016) and Petersen (2016), modified that initial analysis into an analysis of traits or affordances in narratives that stimulate religious use to a higher degree than others (Feldt 2016b). It should be possible to couple this kind of work with the kinds of stories of bodily or interior experiences that Taves and Asprem have been interested in, to see how they stimulate and train experiences, and also to couple the interest in reverse-engineering for experiences-as-events with the interest in the performative mediality and the effectiveness of social frames of the stories-as-narrated. As shown by Geertz and Jensen, religious narrative is one of the fundamental mediating links between individual and collective religious identities (Geertz and Jensen 2011), and for that reason a more detailed analysis and discussion of how narrativity figures in religious experience and identity formation could be fruitful.

Narrativity and Emotion

Stories of fantastic marvels and unusual experiences almost invariably involve emotionality. Emotions also figure prominently in the effects of fantastic stories and stories about unusual experiences. Transgressions of the boundaries of intuitive cognitive domains, ambiguity concerning the status of the fantastic elements, monstrosities, but also simple hyperboles or reversals, and so on (more examples in Feldt 2011, 2017), may offer emotional stimuli related to fear, horror, disorientation, hesitation, and confusion, thus stimulating other responses than our discipline usually attributes to religious narrative (often: belief, trust, consolation, orientation, foundation, and meaning) (Feldt 2011a). As emotions intrinsically form part of experience, I would like to discuss the role of emotion-related aspects of experience, focusing on how understanding experiences-as-events can connect to research on emotions as narrative and on emotions in narratives, and to point to this area as another arena for potential consilience.[4]

Emotions are ubiquitous in narratives. Stories stimulate emotional experiences, feelings, through characters and events, express narrators' feelings, or the emotions of others, and comment on affective processes on a meta-level.[5] Narratives may trigger a broad range of emotional responses in their audiences – a field still under investigation in many disciplines, by cognitive scientists, psychologists, literary scholars, sociologists, and others. Narratives are key in the arousal and shaping of emotions, the somatic and sensory foundations of which are obvious.[6] Emotion researchers today agree that emotions have common cognitive and bodily foundations cross-culturally, and that some degree of universality in human patterns of affective and emotional reaction can be reckoned with.[7] Even as feelings are processes that are historically and

---

4. This section on narrative and the emotions overlaps extensively with my other presentations of intersections between emotionality and narrativity (Feldt 2017; Feldt forthcoming).

5. Scholars disagree as to whether feelings, emotions, and affect are the same thing. Here, I use feelings and emotions as synonyms, while I use the term "affects" to designate the somatic responses. Cf. Hogan for further useful distinctions (Hogan 2011: 2–4), and suffice it to mention here that expressive outcomes, that is, vocalizations of emotion, facial expressions, etc., are also eliciting conditions (p. 3).

6. All kinds of media have the potential to arouse emotions; see Döveling et al. (2011), and Hogan (2011: 1–28).

7. Emotions are often seen as mental and bodily processes with common

culturally very variable, the common cognitive and somatic foundations could give us a workable baseline,[8] if we distinguish between affects as bodily responses and emotions as the verbalized reactions, although this terminology is not uncontested and it is in many ways problematic to set up hard distinctions.[9] Importantly, in my contexts of work, however, is that bodily responses are not naturally meaningful and generally inaccessible to historical research. We might say that we understand affects only when we express, verbalize or narrate them, or in an interplay with a verbalized form (Hogan 2003: 239–64; Scheer 2012; Simecek 2015: 497–500; cf. also Butler 2005; Bourke 2014). The narration of emotions is also key in subject formation and in intersubjective understanding. Narrativization thus influences the processes of emotion and experience stimulation, training and management. This is in line with how some emotion scholars have proposed to understand emotions as events (e.g. Bourke 2014), or indeed, as narratives (Keen 2011; Hogan 2003, 2011), or otherwise closely relate emotions and narratives (Frink 2015). They argue that it is in and through stories and narrative framings that we make sense of emotions, and through narrative that we access the emotions of others and make inferences about them. Following that view and applying it to the study of religions, historically as well as in the contemporary era, entails that we must pay more attention to narrativity and the emotions in the study of religions. So, we need to investigate not only how narratives stimulate emotions but also how emotions unfold narratively[10] and play a role

---

cognitive and somatic foundations, and one view is that the basic emotions (affects) are universal. In the natural sciences, research into the basic emotions is extensive; cf. Paul Ekman who reckons with six basic emotions (Ekman 1972). Important criticism has been voiced especially with regard to whether the data warrant the conclusions; see Döveling *et al.* (2011: 5 with reference to Ekman's work). See also the critical discussion in Hogan (2003); Hogan speaks instead, more convincingly, I believe, of prototypical and culturally widely distributed clusters of emotions.

8. Evolutionary psychology researchers understand emotions as adaptive programs with functional specializations for survival and successful reproduction. There is some work in social psychology on narrative as possessing dynamic structuring techniques for the elicitation of emotions, using film. Social psychology has also described emotional experience as a facet of group membership, and emotion and cognition are generally seen as working together in human bodies (see the details of these discussions in Keen 2011, with references).

9. Others define affect as comprising both moods and emotions, while moods are seen as long-lasting, and emotions as short-lasting and intense (see an overview of the discussions in Barlett and Gentile 2011), but this distinction between affect (or basic emotions) and emotions is nevertheless fairly common (Döveling *et al.* 2011: 3–4).

10. See Geertz and Jensen (2011) for discussions of how memory and identity are also narrative.

in religious identity formation; a complex process that should be studied cross-disciplinarily and in a spirit of consilience.

Important developments in the social sciences, and in research on cognition and affects, have thrown a crucial light on the human emotion systems. Still, many aspects of human emotions cannot be studied by laboratory or cognitive methods, but must be approached with cultural and historical analysis and so the emotions field is ripe for collaboration between natural and humanistic sciences. Historian Joanna Bourke has demonstrated how emotions are socially stimulated, trained, and policed within changing historical and social frames (Bourke 2014) and how that, on the one hand, constrains which emotions are "tellable" for whom, or which ones can gain a social context, it does not, on the other hand, determine emotional responses, as historical changes, negotiations, and challenges to emotional norms also show. Hogan's work is based in the cognitive sciences and discusses how narratives are emotion-based and emotions narrative (2003, 2011). Since emotions are a constitutive part of identity, emotions are key in daily life, in self-narratives and life stories, and since emotions charge situations with personal significance, emotions must be highly important in religious narratives in order to make them effective in social life, for understanding how they become significant in narrative world- and self-making.[11] This means that here too – and especially considering ancient religions – it seems pertinent to ask questions about the performativity of stories, questions from the other end. Key aspects of what makes (religious) narratives – also those about interior experiences – effective as religious media may thus not primarily relate to the belief in the reality of the narrated events, or hark back to an experience-event, but rather, relate to emotional and somatic involvement of their audiences via narrativization (Feldt 2017; Feldt forthcoming).[12] In other words, many of the relevant experiences to analyse might indeed be *in front of* the texts and stories.[13] Even if it is often

---

11. Emotions also play a role in the cultural selection of narratives; they spread and survive related to their effects on memory. I thank Jonas Svensson for this important reminder.

12. The relation, in religious texts, between the narrated events and the authors or redactors can vary from channelling, witnessing, to a visionary or imaginative relationship. As mentioned above, fictionality is not always a problem for religions (Feldt 2011a, 2011b). Indeed, I suggest that the aesthetic form of religious texts and the sensory and emotional stimuli provided – via its aesthetic form, as well as via its usage – are often more important than its propositional content or reality status (Feldt 2017).

13. Here we can connect to my (naturalistic) suggestion that religious narratives can be understood as a subset of fantasy-fictional narratives (Feldt 2006, 2016b, 2017). We should also keep in mind that stories of experiences can be faked; not that they always are, of course, but they *can* be, and still work well as religious expressions.

more pressing, in my areas of work, to ask questions from the other end, as I have indicated here, the focus on narrativity, mediation, and emotion still allows for fruitful connections between cognitive, evolutionary, somatic, history of emotions, narrative and cultural studies approaches, when analysing which types of responses and experiences are cultivated in different religions via differing forms of media and materiality. This could contribute to deeper analyses – and in more areas – of the complex interactions between social and cultural frames and individual cognition and experience.[14]

Religion Everywhere? – Ancient and Contemporary

The final issue I would like to raise regards Taves' and Asprem's suggestion that we use the term "worldview" rather than "religion", or, in other words it regards what we are looking for when we analyse empirical material. In my assessment, we are still better off using a broad concept of religion rather than a concept of worldviews to guide our analyses of the material. I find that a concept of religion as a floating cultural field, as elaborated by Gilhus and Mikaelsson (2001) and discussed further by Sutcliffe and Gilhus (2013) allows us to analyse a broader range of highly interesting things in the field than the term "worldview" does. I would like to point to two exemplary contexts in which "religion", I believe, is more useful than "worldview": religion in ancient Mesopotamia and religion in contemporary popular culture. Neither fits easily with the range of things discussed in depth as examples of (religious) "experience" in Taves (2011) or the examples mentioned in Taves and Asprem (this volume, pp. 5–25 and 2017), and nevertheless they clearly – to my mind – fall within the field of religion.

When Taves and Asprem speak of special paths and paths relative to a goal (2017), one can get the sense that the kinds of religious formations that they have in mind are post-Reformation, modern, and contemporary ones. Yet, some, indeed very many, types of religion – like religion in ancient Mesopotamia – do not have goals relating to salvation or altered states for the individual. Instead, they are more generally focused on survival in the here and now, on maintaining relationships with postulated superhuman beings and powers in order to maintain fertility, health, and security in the field, in the stable, and in bed, and they speak little of special experiences. This holds true of most ancient

---

14. The complex feedback loop formations between cultural frames and cognition and experience is mentioned in Taves 2011 even though bottom-up individual experience is in focus. This question has gained a more prominent position since (Taves and Asprem, BBA paper, p. 8; Taves and Asprem response paper 2017).

temple-based, localistic religions, in which orthopraxy was much more important than orthodoxy and special inner experiences (Johnston 2007). We must be careful to also include types of goals that have nothing to do with interior experience, inner states, salvation, or the like, but which focus on obtaining this-worldly goals – a good harvest, a successful battle, healing for a sick child, and so forth. Some religions display little interest in the interior person, in cultivating special inner experiences, and such experience is not ascribed much importance or reflected in the sources. Most religions-as-lived also include such everyday material aspects and emphases.

Related to this, in the long history of religions we find several contexts in which people do not have an explicit concept of "religion", in which there are no explicit discourses on "religion" to disentangle, and in which religion and culture are fundamentally entwined (as they indeed most commonly are).[15] This is an old truth, and also one, of course, that Taves and Asprem are paying attention to. However, in some contexts it is useful, analytically fruitful, and quite vital to one's work to keep on discussing etic third-order definitions of *religion*; this is also enlightening when they do not fit the material. While it is enlightening to unpack complex CCCs in the work of those scholars who study those religious formations, a concept of religion is arguably still our most fruitful comparative basis for doing so. In order to compare and help us to see where and what to look for in the material, we need "religion". When we then single out things deemed sacred, special, magical, fearsome, awe-inspiring, ritualizing, praise-worthy, taboo, and so on, in a context that does not harbour discourses on "religion", we can only do that by drawing on a long-standing scholarly discussion of religion in our discipline. We need it to guide us when we study fields that have no explicit discourses on religion, magic, or the sacred, for understanding fields such as religion in ancient Mesopotamia, regarding to which a concept of religion or magic can nevertheless be very fruitful to use in order to analyse the sources (cf. Feldt 2015) (just as it would wrong to claim that just because the Mesopotamians did not have a term for mansplaining that we could not find enlightening ways of using that term with regard to their social interactions), but of course "religion" or "the religious" was configured very differently. However, that should be a cause for us to rethink and reconstruct our concept of religion. We need concepts to compare variant religious formations both to gain a deeper knowledge of the different cultures we study, but also to increase our knowledge of the general human phenomena that the term "religion" is used of. I therefore understand concept-based comparison

---

15. Understanding religion as a subset of culture as is commonly done in the study of religions.

as part of our field's constitutive conversation, which is *both* generalizing *and* individualizing in Hartmut Kaelble's sense of the former being interested in establishing general rules of human social life, and the latter in exploring differences (Kaelble 1999: 26; quoted from Stausberg 2011: 32). For such comparative purposes, and considering religion in ancient Mesopotamia, I wager that the concept of religion serves us better than the concept of worldview.

Studies of ancient religions have for some decades now moved away from some of the unfortunate assumptions that seemed to inhere in earlier formulations of the idea of worldviews, especially that they were systematic and coherent, or that singular religious statements could be taken as representative of entire cultures. The ability to move between differing, sometimes conflicting, understandings of reality, space, self, and world is no longer seen as uniquely modern. Ancient, premodern, and indigenous societies can no longer be characterized as static and unchanging. Such views have rightly been abandoned (Petersen and Schjødt 2007). The ability to pendulate between, entertain simultaneously, differing representations of reality, or to use only small parts of worldviews, or to mix them up and shift between them, is, more plausibly, a general, human capacity. So, we cannot speak unproblematically of the ancient Mesopotamian worldview, or the Hebrew worldview, as was once common in these fields, when they were compared (often to the detriment of Mesopotamia, cf. Feldt forthcoming; Feldt 2012b). It would be interesting to see future work on the worldviews approach dialogue explicitly with the research history of the worldviews terminology. Considering the research history of the term worldview, it is hard to escape the connotations that it implies an encompassing, long-lasting, somewhat comprehensive, and, to a certain extent at least, systematic or interconnected view of the world, whereas the term religion can be unfolded in a range of flexible, dynamic, partial and shifting ways that pay attention to its different parts and aspects. To be sure, so can the BBA perhaps, but since the BBA aims to replace the use of concepts of religion, it is worth pointing out what concepts of religion can "do" for us in the discipline. As stressed in the above, the terminology of "building blocks" suggests less emphasis on social context and emergent meanings.

Deconstructions and reconstructions of ancient ways of appraising different phenomena, practices, and experiences is a key concern of studies of ancient religions (cf. recent work: Nongbri 2015; Barton and Boyarin 2016), perhaps precisely because those fields of study do not harbour self-reflective discourses on religion, although some of them, but not all (Feldt 2015), do on "magic" (Stratton 2007). The turn to the study of discourses of religion or magic is basically a good idea, as many studies have shown throughout the last two or three decades or more. Yet, in my assessment, having made that move does not mean that we can stop there. Just because religion and magic and other related concepts form part of emic identity discourses and power plays, they are not invalidated as third-order terms. Indeed, it is actually in some ways an advantage – although in a way that is tricky to handle – that they overlap with contemporary and historical emic terms, because that enhances their value as comparative terms. As outlined briefly above, this is because we compare to gain a greater knowledge about our theoretical object, not to determine a fit. A concept of religion arguably does that better than a concept of "worldview" because it has some resonance with contemporary discourses, and it is easier to use in flexible ways for types of religious formations that do not pay much explicit attention to big questions. Just because concepts are difficult to define or overlap with other concepts does not invalidate them; analytical productivity can sometimes lie in fuzziness and flexibility. The term religion can be unfolded in a range of flexible and dynamic ways, if we understand it to also encompass very practical concerns of everyday life, as well as spirituality, seeking, and so on. I would like to unfold this more in relation to another field of inquiry of mine, namely religion, media and popular culture.

When investigating "religion" in contemporary media and popular culture we see developments that do not have much to do with worldviews or capital-R religion classically understood. It cannot be fitted into neat and separate boxes – one religion here, another one there, or religion here, entertainment there. Like other contemporary religious formations, for instance New Age spiritualities (Sutcliffe and Gilhus 2013), religion in the popular culture field must be grasped in a different way. Religion is here mediated and disseminated via popular media, religious references and vocabulary are thinly spread out, and thoroughly mixed with other things like entertainment, commerce, and play (Gilhus and Mikaelsson 2001, 2005; Feldt 2016a, 2016b; Undheim 2018). As I have previously argued, while the Harry Potter novels fall within the field of religion, because they are inserted into discourses on religion by various actors, they also fall within the field because of the way the novels are construed as media, because of their mediality, their vocabulary and their content (Feldt 2016a, 2016b, 2017). Nevertheless, in the western world, in popular response, the Harry Potter phenomenon is often *not* labelled as belonging to the field of religion by most actors. It flies under the radar of common conceptions of "religion", and it is also not necessarily representative or formative of worldviews, even though it participates in the religious field. Popular culture multi-media super-systems such as Harry Potter, *Game of Thrones*, or Lego Chima not only reflect but contribute to ongoing religious change and religious story-telling in contemporary societies (Partridge 2004–2006; Endsjø and Lied 2011; Undheim

2018), even as they remain far from standard conceptions of capital-R religion. Just because the Danish preoccupation with gnomes, decorated trees, Disney cartoons, and fat foods one week before New Year's day is labelled "hygge", does not mean that those activities have nothing to do with religion. For such areas of study, just as for ancient Mesopotamia, a broad concept of religion as a floating cultural field allows us to distinguish between different expressions, parts, practices, and aspects that are systematic and coherent to *varying* degrees: capital R religions, religious movements, informal religious networks, thinly spread out religious representations, narratives, and vocabulary – that is, we can work from a concept of a broad cultural field, within which we can find "religion" in very different ways, stratified contexts, amounts, combinations, and aspects. We need an etic, third-order perspective in order to understand such phenomena and contexts; contexts that fly under the radar of many actors as not-religion, that are commonly appraised as entertainment, commerce, play or family tradition instead. And we need to use an *explicit* concept of religion – because otherwise we'll just be using an implicit one and occlude intersubjective discussion and testing. "Religion" thinly spread out in terms of free-floating expressions, vocabulary, partial mythologies, or one-off performances or rapidly shifting practices, shifting attitudes to religion, and partial engagements in "religion" are also parts of the category of "religion", understanding that term to also encompass for instance what actors in the field might call "spirituality", "entertainment", or "magic". The understanding of religion as a unitary, organizationally defined, and relatively stable set of beliefs, experiences, and practices clearly falls short of both contemporary and historical developments in the realm of popular and lived religion, but then we'll just have to broaden and refine the concept. Looking only at how things are appraised or labelled *as religious* – which features as a key part of Taves and Asprem's approach (this volume, pp. 5–25), or at worldviews, as they also suggest, could obscure many aspects of how the field works in partial, thinly spread out, or mixed-up ways. The current popularity of religiously tinged experiences of consuming religious mystery, titillation and fascination in multi-media fantasy fiction, in combination with the use of related virtual worlds that do not hark back to any original experiences, indicate that such fiction- and fantasy-based experiences have a broader social significance today, but historical examples are also ample (Feldt 2011a, 2016b). This indicates to me that it would be relevant for historians of religion if the BBA would also address explicitly made-up stories. I would like to end with the suggestion or wager that the broad range of flexible terminology that the concept of "religion" opens up – Religions, religions, religion, the religious, and the religious field – remains more versatile for more different kinds of material from the long history of religions, from the very ancient to the very recent. Moreover, these terms enable us to keep up an enormously fascinating scholarly conversation in our discipline that we can still learn a lot from.

About the Author

Laura Feldt is Associate Professor of the study of religions with the University of Southern Denmark, editor-in-chief of *Numen - International Review of the History of Religions* with G. D. Alles, author of *The Fantastic in Religious Narrative from Exodus to Elisha* (2012a), editor of *Reframing Authority - the Role of Media and Materiality* (with C. Høgel, 2018), and *Marginality, Media, and Mutations of Religious Authority in the History of Christianity* (with J. N. Bremmer, 2019). Her research interests include – among others – ancient religions, monstrosities, fantastic stories, wilderness mythologies, and contemporary popular culture.

References

Barlett, Christopher P., and Douglas A. Gentile. 2011. "Affective and Emotional Consequences of the Mass Media." In *The Routledge Handbook of Emotions and Mass Media*, edited by Katrin Döveling, Christian von Scheve, and Ellie A. Konijn, 60–78. London: Routledge.

Barton, C., and D. Boyarin. 2016. *Imagine No Religion: How Modern Abstractions Hide Ancient Realities.* New York: Fordham University Press.

Bourke, Joanna. 2014. *The Story of Pain: From Prayer to Painkillers.* Oxford: Oxford University Press.

Butler, Judith. 2005. *Giving an Account of Oneself.* New York: Fordham University Press.

Davidsen, Markus. 2016. "The Religious Affordance of Fiction: A Semiotic Approach." *Religion* 46(4): 521–49.

Döveling, Katrin, Christian von Scheve, and Ellie A. Konijn, eds. 2011. *The Routledge Handbook of Emotions and Mass Media.* London: Routledge.

Ekman, Paul. 1972. "Universals and Cultural Differences in Facial Expressions of Emotion." In *Nebraska Symposion on Motivation 1971*, edited by James Cole, 207–82. Lincoln: University of Nebraska Press.

Endsjø, D. Ø., and L. I. Lied. 2011. *Det folk vil ha. Religion og populærkultur.* Oslo: Universitetsforlaget.

Fauconnier, G., and M. Turner. 2002. *The Way We Think.* New York: Basic Books.

Feldt, Laura. 2006. "Signs of Wonder – Traces of Doubt: The Fantastic in the Exodus Narrative." In *Fremde Wirklichkeiten: Literarische Phantastik und antike Literatur*, edited by N. Hömke and M. Baumbach, 311–38. Heidelberg: Universitätsverlag Winter.

—2011a. "Religious Narrative and the Literary Fantastic: Ambiguity and Uncertainty in Ex 1–18." *Religion* 41(2): 251–83.

—2011b. "Fantastic Re-Collection: Cultural vs. Autobiographical Memory in the Exodus Narrative." In *Religious Narrative, Cognition and Culture: Image and Word*

in the Mind of Narrative, edited by A. W. Geertz and J. S. Jensen, 191–208. London: Equinox.
—2012a. *The Fantastic in Religious Narrative from Exodus to Elisha*. London: Routledge.
—2012b. "Wilderness and Hebrew Bible Religion – Fertility, Apostasy and Religious Transformation in the Pentateuch." In *Wilderness in Mythology and Religion: Approaching Religious Spatialities, Cosmologies and Ideas of Wild Nature*, edited by L. Feldt, 55–94. Berlin: Walter de Gruyter.
—2015. "Monstrous Figurines from Mesopotamia." In *The Materiality of Magic*, edited by Jan N. Bremmer and Dietrich Boschung, 59–96. Paderborn: Vilhelm Fink.
—2016a. "Harry Potter and Contemporary Magic – Fantasy Literature, Popular Culture, and the Representation of Religion." *Journal of Contemporary Religion* 31(1): 101–14.
—2016b. "Contemporary Fantasy Fiction and Representations of Religion: Playing with Reality, Myth and Magic in his Dark Materials and Harry Potter." *Religion* 46(4): 550–74.
—2016c. "Myth, Space, and the History of Religions: Reflections on the Comparative Study of Wilderness Mythologies from Mesopotamia, the Hebrew Bible, and Early Christianity." In *Contemporary Views on Comparative Religion*, edited by Peter Antes, Armin W. Geertz, and Michael Rothstein, 85–97. London: Equinox Publishing.
—2017. "The Literary Aesthetics of Religious Narratives: Probing Literary-Aesthetic Form, Emotion, and Sensory Effects in Exodus 7–11." In *The Aesthetics of Religion: A Connective Concept*, edited by Alexandra A. Grieser and Jay Johnston, 121–44. Berlin: Walter de Gruyter.
—Forthcoming. "Narrative Cultures and the Stimulation of Emotions." In *Narrative Cultures and the Aesthetics of Religion*, edited by Dirk Johannsen et al. Method and Theory in the Study of Religion Book Series. Leiden: Brill.
Feldt, L., and C. Høgel, eds. 2018. *Reframing Authority: The Role of Media and Materiality*. London: Equinox.
Frink, Stephanie. 2015. "The Past Beats inside me Like a Second Heart." *Structures of Feeling: Affectivity and the Study of Culture*, edited by Devika Sharma and Frederik Tygstrup, 132–46. Berlin: Walter de Gruyter.
Geertz, Armin W. 1999. "Definition as Analytical Strategy in the Study of Religion." *Historical Reflections/Réflexions Historiques* 25(3): 445–75.
Geertz, A. W., and J. S. Jensen, eds. 2011. *Religious Narrative, Cognition and Culture: Image and Word in the Mind of Narrative*. London: Equinox.
Gilhus, Ingvild S., and Lisbeth Mikaelsson. 2001. *Nyt blikk på religion: Studiet af religion i dag*. Oslo: Pax.
—2005. *Kulturens refortrylling: Nyreligiøsitet i modern samfunn*. Oslo: Universitetsforlaget.
Hogan, Patrick Colm. 2003. *The Mind and its Stories*. Cambridge: Cambridge University Press.
—2011. *Affective Narratology: The Emotional Structure of Stories*. London/Lincoln: University of Nebraska Press.
Jensen, J. Sinding. 2009. "Explanation and Interpretation in the Comparative Study of Religion." *Religion* 39(4): 331–39.
Jensen, J. Sinding. 2003. *The Study of Religion in a New Key: Theoretical and Philosophical Soundings in the Comparative and General Study of Religion*. Aarhus: Aarhus University Press.
Johnston, S. I. ed. 2007. *Ancient Religions*. Cambridge, MA: Harvard University Press.

Kaelble, H. 1999. *Der historische Vergleich. Eine Einführung zum 19. und 20. Jahrhundert.* Campus Verlag: Frankfurt a.M.

Keen, Suzanne. 2011. "Emotions and Narrative." *Poetics Today* 32(1): 1–53.

Nongbri, Brent. 2015. *Before Religion: A History of a Modern Concept.* New Haven, CT: Yale University Press.

Partridge, Christopher. 2004–2006. *The Re-Enchantment of the West. Alternative Spiritualities, Sacralization, Popular Culture and Occulture*, Vols. I-II. London: T&T Clark.

Petersen, Anders K. 2016. "The Relationship between Religious Narratives and Fictional Narratives: A Matter of Degree Only." *Religion* 46(4): 500–20.

Petersen, A. K., and J.-P. Schjødt. 2007. "Balkanisering og rekonstruktion af kulturer." *Religionsvidenskabeligt Tidsskrift* 50: 7–9.

Ricoeur, Paul. 1965. *De l'interprétation. Essai sur Freud.* Paris: Éditions du Seuil.

—1975. *La métaphore vive.* Paris: Éditions du Seuil.

Schaffalitzky de Muckadell, Caroline. 2014. "On Real and Essential Definitions in the Study of Religions." *Journal of the American Academy of Religion* 82: 495–520.

Scheer, Monique. 2012. "Are Emotions a Kind of Practice (and is That What Makes Them Have a History)? A Bourdieuian Approach to Understanding Emotion." *History and Theory* 51(2): 193–220.

Segal, Robert A. 2006. "All Generalizations are Bad: Postmodernism on Theories." *Journal of the American Academy of Religion* 74(1): 157–71.

Simecek, Karen. 2015. "Beyond Narrative: Poetry, Emotion, and the Perspectival View." *British Journal of Aesthetics* 55(4): 497–513.

Stausberg, Michael. 2011. "Comparison." In *The Routledge Handbook of Research Methods in the Study of Religion*, edited by Michael Stausberg and Steven Engler, 21–39. London: Routledge.

Stratton, Kimberley. 2007. *Naming the Witch: Gender, Ideology and Stereotype in the Ancient World.* New York: Columbia University Press.

Sutcliffe, Steven, and Ingvild S. Gilhus. 2013. "Introduction: All Mixed Up – Thinking about Religion in Relation to New Age Spiritualities." In *New Age Spirituality: Rethinking Religion*, edited by Steven J. Sutcliffe and Ingvild S. Gilhus, 1–16. London: Acumen.

Taves, Ann. 2011 [2009]. *Religious Experience Reconsidered: A Building-Block Approach to the Study of Religion and Other Special Things.* Princeton, NJ: Princeton University Press.

Taves, Ann, and Egil Asprem. 2017. "Experience as Event: Event Cognition and the Study of (Religious) Experiences." *Religion, Brain & Behaviour* 7(1): 43–62.

Undheim, Sissel. 2018. "Lego Religion in the Classroom. The Potential Use of Children's Popular Culture in the Teaching of Religion in Kindergarten and Primary School." *Didaktik/Didactique, Zeitschrift für Religionskunde - Revue de didactique des sciences des religions* 6: 52–66.

4

Counterintuitive Supernaturalism as a Building Block of Religious Dream Imagery

Andreas Nordin
University of Gothenburg

Introduction

Based on reports from various parts of the world, scholars have proposed the notion that dreaming is the primary source of religion. A fairly strong case might be made for the argument that supernaturalistic cognition prevails in dreaming processes occurring in cultural environments rich in religious representations. This chapter outlines a moderate defence of the anchoring function of supernaturalism by suggesting that counterintuitive properties in dream imagery are prevalent tendencies and decisive building blocks, rendering these representations relevant and salient and giving them a special status in religious institutionalization. I will draw from cross-cultural research and Hindu Nepalese ethnography to support the argument.

Piecemeal, Building-block, and Fractionated Religion

Anthropologically speaking, religion is not a unitary phenomenon (e.g. Bloch 2008; Boyer 2013; Sperber 2017) but rather forms a polythetic cluster made up of more basic and recurrent traits that do not co-occur in every cultural environment. Rather than attempting to explain a presumed cohesive category, this chapter starts from the methodological assumption that religion is a fragmented entity encompassing a broad range of different phenomena that should be "fractionated" into constitutive parts better suited for scientific investigation (e.g. Atran 2002; Boyer 2001, 2005; Sørensen 2005). This is a kind of "piecemeal" (Barret 2007) or "building-block" (Taves 2011) approach to the research areas, one that explores targeted exemplars that are seemingly related in cause or effect regardless of any purported coherence of these items. This type of approach is generally part and parcel of the broader research programme of the cognitive and evolutionary science of religion. Although the "building-block approach" (BBA) is very much in line with standard accounts in the subfields of cognitive and evolutionary science of religion and their fractionated take on religion, it can be argued that it also contributes to reaching out to a broader audience in the study of religion and culture. The BBA further constructs a partly novel methodological nomenclature. Although "hardcore" scholars in the slightly heterogeneous research programme of cognitive and evolutionary science of religions and related fields in cognitive anthropology grant basic assumptions of the BBA, they may also sense that the approach to some extent is forcing an open door. Further, in doing so the BBA is perhaps not fully acknowledging the numerous other theories and scholars in the field that over the last decades have made similar proposals and initiated similar methodologies (among others, Atran 2002; Boyer 2001, 2005; Barrett 2007; Sørensen 2005). Methodologically, supernatural dreams can be analysed as instances of the cultural occurrence of supernatural agent concepts that most likely involve counterintuitive processing. This approach suggests that counterintuition is strongly connected to clusters of interrelated religious-making characteristics. In the case of dreaming, however, not all dream content is counterintuitive, as was suggested in Brereton's (2000: 400) "social mapping hypothesis", wherein dreaming is held to share core features with symbolization, such as counterintuitive properties, and which implies that all (social) dreaming would be counterintuitive.

The Scope of an Analytical Category of "Religious" Dreaming

My own research presupposes the partly empirical hypothesis that counterintuitive dreaming is rather fundamental in supernatural and purportedly religious dream imagery. Methodologically, the present approach to "religious" dreaming suggests that the term "religious" is shorthand for a conglomerate of disparate parts, phenomena, processes, and causes. This invites a combination of interrelated research domains and prominent theories in the naturalistic research programme relating culture, cognition, and religion. In that sense, "religious" dreaming draws upon the same neurocognitive mechanisms as ordinary dreaming and cognitive processing. In particular, it draws upon cognitive machinery suggested in Threat Simulation Theory, whereby dreaming is an evolved cognitive capacity that helps people to simulate threatening events, rehearse threat perception and enhance threat avoidance (Revonsuo 2000); in dream-prediction approaches (e.g. Llewellyn 2015; McNamara and Bulkeley 2015); in agent detection approaches (e.g. Barrett 2004); and in counterintuitiveness approaches (see below). "Religious" and supernatural dreaming arguably involve salient emotional and counterintuitive contents and appraisals that enhance memorability and are canalized as "special" narratives. These are anchored as emotionally convincing trust, truth, and sacred value (related to disbelief in purely bizarre dreams), with an automatic affordance capacity supporting a readiness for further ritualization and cultural institutionalization taking the form of expertise, exegetic models and modus operandi.

Institutionalization and Specialness-attribution in Religious-making Characteristics

Alleged religious items are treated according to an axiology of specialness, although the elusive property of specialness certainly is conceivable in most of the cognitive processing and social interaction that humans undertake. In this context, a complementary way to explicate a Durkheimian approach to sacredness or specialness construals (cf. Antonnen 1996; e.g. Sørenson 2007; Taves 2011) is to suggest that these notions belong to a subclass of a broader category of cultural institutionalization where people recognize and accept that certain persons, events and things must be treated in a stipulated way because of an assumed objective or natural property of that person, event or thing (e.g. D'Andrade 2002: 63). At the same time, such a Durkheimian approach would not point to any "unique" religiousness-making characteristics, but to phenomena recurrent in all sociocultural niches and institutions. Certainly, cultural and cognitive institutional mechanisms operate in both the stipulation of religious items, experience and behaviours, and the conglomerate of social formations built from such items. From the perspective of a naturalized ontology, institutions are generally understood without asserting any extra, non-naturalistic entities or domains of socially constructed reality (Boyer and Petersen 2011), making reference instead to individual belief-events and cognition (Searle 1995, 2005). Accordingly, institutions constitute and implement certain types of facts, where X (a person, object or condition) is reckoned as Y (a special status property) in situation Z, wherein X, with the help of Y, can exercise specific social functions, rights or duties (Searle 2005). Interestingly, as social-cognitive mechanisms, institutions include the causes of self-maintenance (e.g. Barnes 1983; Searle 1995; Sperber 1996; cf. Heintz 2007), and regulation of behaviour and possible action. Not surprisingly, it is suggested here that religious items are just another subcategory that is subject to these mechanisms.

Supernatural Imagery as Building Blocks of Religious Dream Imagery

The anthropological and religious-studies literature demonstrates that in traditional societies dreaming, dream experience, and narrative are connected with religious ideas and practices (e.g. Tylor 1871; Tedlock 1987; Jedrej and Shaw 1992; Doniger and Bulkeley 1993; Lohmann 2003; Mageo 2003; Bulkeley 2007, 2008; Laughlin 2011). The ethnographic literature points to the widespread cultural value attached to supernatural agent concepts and dreams (Jedrej and Shaw 1992; Littlewood 2004; Peluso 2004; Renne 2004) and their importance in all the world's religious traditions (Doniger and Bulkeley 1993; Bulkeley 2007, 2008, 2009). The prominence of religious dreams has been observed in studies of Taliban Jihadists (Edgar 2004), independent churches in Nigeria (Renne 2004), Trinidadian Baptists (Littlewood 2004), and Jewish nationalism (Knafo and Glick 2000). Several scholars suggest that dreaming is a primary source of religion in traditional cultures (e.g. Tylor 1871; Tedlock 1987) and furthermore that dreams are useful tools for spreading religious ideas (Knafo and Glick 2000). Indeed, early anthropological accounts in Tylor (1871) suggested that dreaming was the experiential source of religious beliefs, based on the observation of the nearly universal belief that dreams involve experiences of and communication with "real" souls, spirits, ancestors, gods, and other supernatural entities. These observations and suggestions prompt the use of a BBA in which supernatural and counterintuitive (below) imagery is a recurrent pattern. The uses of dreams illustrate the value attached to supernatural agent concepts (e.g. Jedrej and Shaw 1992; Peluso 2004; Renne 2004), but these descriptions also lack a theory-driven understanding of the structure, content, and distribution of the cognitive cultural schemas, scripts, and emotions associated with religious dreaming.

One tendency seen in the literature on religious dreaming is the likelihood that early human populations (and probably human populations ever since) deployed dreams as *evidence* for supernatural entities and realms, in that such convictions were based on *vivid emotional experience* and a sense of "realness", and on an *involuntary encounter* with a supernatural agent. Such data is cross-culturally manifested in apparitions and "visitations" – dreams that combine an intense sense of reality with a strongly apprehensive or non-apprehensive experience. In most traditions, dreams tend to be accorded status and value as markers of some special conditions (see institutionalization). Further, some scholars argue that the importance of such experiences is recurrent in all the world's religious traditions (e.g. Doniger and Bulkeley 1993; Bulkeley 2007, 2008). Furthermore, the recurrent tendency to attribute a value of specialness manifests the culturally widespread notion of dreams as anchors of belief by offering experiential verification and evidence of the existence of religious entities and spirit realms (Bulkeley 2008). Similar results in the ethnographical literature from cross-cultural surveys of dreams also highlight the importance of cultural traits that relate dreams to religious systems (D'Andrade 1961). There is widespread use of dreams to contact or gain control of supernatural powers (agents) as well as beliefs about the soul wandering during sleep and meeting other souls. D'Andrade's (pp. 320, 328) study further shows that anxiety about being alone, expectations of self-reliance, and isolation give rise to powerful preoccupation with dreams. In many traditions and cultures, it is held that the dreamer's soul visits the spirit world and communes with gods and spirits (e.g. Lohmann 2003). Importantly, in various cultures and religious traditions, dreams and nightmares are employed by shamans, healers, prophets, and oracles in local rituals, pilgrimage cults, initiations, and conversion ordeals (Morinis 1982; Bulkeley 2007; Nordin 2011).

Nightmares are often held to be warnings from spirits, ancestors, God or the gods, or demons. Ethnographic descriptions from several cultures in which ancestor worship is common practice also note that dead ancestors appear in frightening and memorable dreams to reprimand the dreamer for failing to perform commemorative rituals (e.g. Trompf 1990; Jedrej and Shaw 1992; Boyer 2001).

Neurocognitive Underpinnings of Supernatural Imagery

One way to contribute to a broader and more profound understanding of the complexity of supernatural imagery considered as religious building blocks is to use prominent models from the neurocognitive literature. Although most dreams seem to occur during REM (rapid eye movement) sleep, the mind-brain system is active during the whole sleep cycle, indicating that we dream more or less all night long (Bulkeley 2007), during the NREM (non-rapid eye movement) sleep state (e.g. McNamara and Bulkeley 2015). During REM sleep, several distinct physiological and neurological conditions occur such as discharges in the autonomic nervous system and release of certain hormones, muscle paralysis and/or various muscle jolting, and changeability in blood pressure and heart rate, while at the same time the limbic region and the amygdala in particular are highly activated (detailed account in McNamara and Bulkeley 2015; McNamara 2016). As summarized by McNamara and Bulkeley (2015), during REM sleep there is furthermore a deactivation of the dorsolateral prefrontal cortex, the locus coeruleus, and the noradrenergic and serotonergic systems, in addition to activation of the dopaminergic and cholinergic circuits (also, e.g., Maque *et al.* 1996; Hobson *et al.* 1998). One consequence of the complex co-occurrence of these brain activities during sleep states is the seeming provision for the more intricate cognitive process of supernatural agent concepts. There is a manifest difference both in dream content and experience between REM and NREM states, such that the former peak in negative emotions, nightmarish threat scenery and bizarre imagery, while the latter manifest the opposite tendency (e.g. Hall and Van de Castle 1966; Revonsuo 2000). For example, McNamara *et al.* demonstrate that scored aggression levels were lowest in NREM and waking reports, as compared to REM-sleep, and the imagery of friendliness signifies NREM states (2010). The correlation between apprehensive/non-apprehensive imagery and REM and NREM states also suggests that the supernatural dream content is heavily affected. Indeed, various types of demonic, threatening, and predatory supernatural imagery prevail in REM states, while properties of non-apprehensiveness friendliness and love characterize NREM imagery (Bulkeley 2007; Nordin 2011; McNamara and Bulkeley 2015).

As indicated from the frequency of nightmares and apprehensive dreams, the dreamers' own agency is highly impeded or absent during REM sleep. The experience in the dreamer of a sense of reduced personal agency or suspension of an acting self-model may account for an increased sense of the causal agentive role attributed to other special dream characters (McNamara and Bulkeley 2015; McNamara 2016). According to models such as the predictive coding approach (e.g. Howhy 2013; Clark 2016), or types of dream prospective coding (Llewellyn 2013, 2015) or the simulation approach (Valli and Revonsuo 2009), cognitive processes in the brain, grossly simplified, strive to confirm the brains own prospective states, actions and thought. Consequently, the experience of being in charge of one's own actions, mental process and sensory events derives from automatic and comparative processes between predicted and intended outcomes, such that if there is a match, the experience of self-causation increases, while a mismatch between predictions and actual outcome encourages attribution of external causal agency (McNamara and Bulkeley 2015).

During the REM dreaming, there is a downregulation of activation and intention and hence a predictive gap, a condition that may suggest that the dreamer tests a model whereby cues of dream agency are interpreted as coming from causal sources and characters external to the perspective of the dream ego (McNamara and Bulkeley 2015). Furthermore, according to McNamara and Bulkeley, the prerequisite for the production of highly memorable supernatural agent (SA) dreams is the same as that for the generation of ordinary SA concepts or God concepts, and involves mental simulation of alternate beings/realities, theory of mind (ToM) attribution, and reckoning of extreme or ultimate values (2015).

These conditions would suggest that we are endowed with a mind-brain system innately primed to regularly generate supernatural agent concepts in dreaming. However, such a proposal raises questions about why not everyone's dreams contain SA images, whether non-believers' dreams contain these images, and the extent to which devotees in any religious system have dreams filled with SA imagery. Furthermore, why should counterintuitive (below) SA dreaming be limited to allegedly religious correlates?

Supernaturalism and Cultural Selection Factors

The previous discussion suggests that counterintuition, besides bringing strong and vivid emotions, improves memorability, salience, and the inferential potential of religious dreams, rendering these representations successful in cultural transmission and selection. Consequently, counterintuitive aspects are what you remember and can communicate about with others after you wake up. The fact that certain cultural environments ascribe higher value to supernaturalist imagination and representation is highly indicative of the presence of schemas supporting the memorability and transmission advantage of the dreams. The previous discussion may offer additional force to observations about the proneness to attribute dream agency, although it does not completely explain why *supernatural* and counterintuitive agency would be a preferred imaginary construct in religious dreaming. Importantly, we may ask whether the process connected to religious dreaming somehow overproduces counterintuitive imagery, or whether cultural and religious schemata provide an evaluative and conceptual context that enhances memorability, attention and hence the selection and attraction of counterintuitive SA concepts. Furthermore, the cognitive account of counterintuitive SA concepts and the alleged cultural selection advantage of these notions is also one explanation for why these items are recurrent and deserve to be labelled building blocks.

Supernatural Agent Imagery and Minimal Counterintuitiveness Theory and Building Blocks of Religious Dreaming

From these cases it is obvious not only that the trait of supernaturalism can be viewed as a pervasive building block in allegedly religious dreams, but also, and more profoundly, such dreams are likely to be instances of a culturally variable repertoire of SA concepts involving counterintuitive processing.

This suggests the argument that: (a) counterintuitive processing in supernatural dream imagery is a decisive building block of allegedly religious dreaming; and (b) these dreams are a distinct building block of purportedly religious experience and traditions. Most cognitive approaches seem unable to account for why seemingly religious dreaming should (a) contain *manifest* SA imagery and (b) *manifest* counterintuitive properties of SA dream imagery. Still, some sort of counterintuitive processing is likely to prevail in religious dreams, and such conditions may explain the institutionalization and specialness-making of these types of dreams and of these items' allegedly constitutional status in religious traditions and sociocultural formations. The core idea of minimal counterintuitiveness (MCI) theory is the notion of counterintuition, which refers to violations of intuitive expectation, such as breaches and transfers of basic ontological categories (e.g. Boyer 1994, 2001; Barrett 2000, 2004; Pyysiäinen 2001). For a more comprehensive review of the literature see Barrett (2008), Purzycki and Willard (2016), and Pyysiäinen (2009). Such breaches and transfers hypothetically render (minimally) counterintuitive concepts *cognitively optimal* in cultural transmission and communication (Boyer and Ramble 2001). MCI theorists usually claim that cognitively optimal counterintuitive ideas form the backbone of significant traits in the cluster of religious phenomena and traditions, and they offer explanations for the recurrence of certain types of concepts as resulting from cultural and cognitive selection. Still, MCI theory does not aim to account for religious concepts as a kind of demarcated natural domain of concepts (e.g. Barrett 2017).

In order to tackle the problem of measuring and quantifying counterintuitive properties in religious representation, Barrett (2008) has constructed a procedure of specification that enables the quantification of types and degrees of counterintuitiveness (CI) and the making of predictions about the transmission advantage of counterintuitive items. Barrett's strategy is also compatible with the BBA. Accordingly, the CI scheme enables predictions about the transmission advantage of score 1 counterintuitiveness, namely that higher-scoring counterintuitive breaches are likely to be re-represented in simpler and less counterintuitive forms, and there will be a tendency toward metonymic transfer, such that a transferred property will encourage the assumption that the whole set of properties is transferred. Coding and identifying counterintuitive concepts entails coding public representations of their probable private/mental representational structures (e.g. Sperber 1996) and further, since it is likely that human minds generally strive for relevance and computational simplicity and efficiency (Sperber and Wilson 1995) we should employ a *simplicity rule* regarding the way people conceptualize counterintuitive representations, and assume that the simplest and least counterintuitive concepts are employed (Barrett 2008). Then we enter into the following six step-procedure. The simplest and least counterintuitive concepts are employed (Barrett 2008). Then we enter into the following six step-procedure. First, identify the basic level category membership in the counterintuitive representation. Second identify the ontological category(ies) of the counterintuitive representation, such as spatiality, physicality, biology, animacy, mentality (theory of mind), and universals. Third, *transfers* of counterintuition in a given item are to be coded with an inserted capitalized prefix joined by + if necessary; for example, *Bhagawan* (Hindu God) manifesting in a gigantic stone pig speaking human language and offering advice and blessings is to be coded as "STATUE" (= Solid Object + Biology + Mentality) = $^{B(iology) +M(entality)}$ **STATUE**. Fourth, code the counterintuitive *breaches* of expectation as Superscript Lowercase Suffixes, for example, *Invisible Mountain* (breaches of expectations of physicality). This item may be coded as Rock (or Mountain) = ROCK $^{P(hysicality)}$. Combining steps 3 and 4 (transfer and breaches), for example, *Growing and invisible statue* (transfer of expectation of Biology and breaches of expectations of Physicality). Coded as Statue = $^{B(iology)}$STATUE $^{P(hysicality)}$.

Support for Counterintuitive Dream Content – the Hindu Nepalese Case

The importance of counterintuitive dream contents can be supported by further empirical data from my ethnographic research in Nepal during 2016, which aimed to address the prevalence of allegedly counterintuitive dream imagery. In the study, Hindu-Nepali informants from the Pokhara and Kathmandu valleys were interviewed about the specific content of dreams they *considered to be* and *remembered as* "special" and represented in dream narratives at religious sites (e.g. "Mandir" and "Tirtha") and nonreligious sites. In total 61 interviews were conducted with 39 males (63.9%) and 22 females (36.1%). The interviews were based on a Qualtrics questionnaire that took approximately two hours to complete. The questionnaire covered a broad range of topics such as dream content, social use, emotionality scores, religiosity scores, and dream rationalizations.

The rough statistics from this study demonstrate a high prevalence of direct or indirect counterintuitive imagery. For the sake of empirical and phenomenological clarity, it is valuable to offer a real-life ethnographic depiction about what is actually going on in these religious dreams and the content from whose narrative context the dreams derive. Below are some examples demonstrating how and to what extent supernaturalism and counterintuitive content occur in dream reports.

The first example of a dream narrative contains one counterintuitive transfer of animacy to an artefact or object coded as ^{A}**Artefact** from the underscored section in the quote:

> I was going back ... home (Bihar) on a long bus with my other villagers. At the bus stop all the people got [off] ... and I was sleeping. After some time, someone came to the driver's seat[1] and took the bus to the sky by driving into the air (flying) ... (and) the bus stopped at *Sworga* (heaven) there were many *Bhagwans* (deities), but I couldn't remember their faces. It was

---

1. Note on transcription error: I here use "driver's seat" instead of the incoherent transcription "driver seated".

a different world. All were sitting like a single family, reading books, chanting mantras (sacred syllables). I went to the corner, listened and watched them curiously. At the same time the place was full of light and I felt like I had fallen [out of] ... bed and got up screaming on my bed. My wife got up and gave me a glass of water.

The second example of a dream narrative contains several counterintuitive fragments such as breaches of universality in an artefact/object – **Bowl**^{u}; transfer of the physical property of generating combustion to a person – ^{P}**Agent**; a breach where the dead come to life – ^{B}**Corpse**, seen in the underscored sections in the quote:

> Among many dreams the dream that I like to talk most about is: a beggar wearing grey clothes and asking for rice/money who came to my house. I went inside my house and took a bowl of rice from a basket and [poured it] ... into his bag but the small bowl didn't empty. The bag was full and the bowl was also empty. I got surprised [went] ... inside again, opened the basket, but it was full [of] ... *Shaligram* (sacred ammonite fossils, usually believed to the relics of and animated by the deity *Vishnu Narayan*) and flowers. I could see *mandirs* (temples) and rivers inside the basket where *Bhagwans* were singing and dancing. I went and joined [the] *Bhagwans* and *Devetas* there. I was like a friend to them. They put me on a bamboo stretcher and threw [me] into the water. My legs and body [were tied] with a *Nag* (supernatural serpent). I could do nothing after that, I was put on a block of firewood. Some unknown people (actually could not remember what is was) produced fire from the mouth and set fire to the firewood. I was burnt and died. The fire went out and again I got off the block of firewood and came down, nothing has happened to my body, I was surprised in the dream too.

Manifest and explicit counterintuitive imagery were common and we identified explicit counterintuitive imagery in 70.5% of the dreams reported, and it occurred in 43 out of 61 analysed reports. The counterintuitive content was manifest in the sense that the markers of counterintuition were unprompted and mentioned spontaneously by the informants. Manifest counterintuitive dream content was contrasted with indirect counterintuitive dream content (where the informant describes the properties of the supernatural agent in his/her dream using a theologically correct mode of cognition similar to what is seen in off-line reasoning). Examples of manifest counterintuitive dream content can be seen in quotes such as: "Bhagwan (God/the Lord) appeared as a half murti (statue)/half man offering advice"; "Bhagwan appeared as a statue talking to me like a human" "a big Nag (supernatural serpent) appeared, whispering", and so on.

Adopting Barrett's procedure for specifying types and degrees of counterintuitiveness we see that mental representations may in principle contain from zero to several counterintuitive breaches or transfers. However, the simplicity rule tells us: "When coding concepts, assume the simplest (i.e. least counterintuitive) conceptual representation that captures the object's properties" (Barrett 2008: 316). The simplicity rule would suggest that we methodologically choose the least complex representations with the fewest violations of intuitive expectations when analysing data.

As stated above a simplicity rule regarding the way people conceptualize counterintuitive representations, assumes that the simplest and least counterintuitive concepts are employed (Barrett 2008). It is thus primarily a methodological precept based on the condition of human cognition. It implies that the inferential potential of these representations presumably peaks with a counterintuitiveness score of 1–2. This alleged "peak" of the score at 1-2 breaches is predicted by the simplicity rule and is confirmed empirically (above). Concepts with a higher counterintuitiveness score than 2 seem to require additional support (e.g. rituals, teaching, and theology) to be transmitted (Barrett 2008: 327). The score thus measures the number of counterintuitive breaches that occur in a concept. For example, a concept with one counterintuitive breach is recognized as having a score of 1.

In the present instance, a score of 1 for manifest counterintuitive imagery occurred in 35 cases (57.4%) while a score of 2 occurred in 11 cases. This would suggest that Barrett's approach is correct. Further, in the dream reports, counterintuition according to the principle of *transfer* occurred in 27 cases (44.3%), and as breaching in 12 cases (12.7%). Some of the most common types of score 1 representations were dreams about communicating statues (8), bodiless voices (9), flying beds/buses (2), resurrection/re-existence (3), moving statues (2), impossible artefacts (e.g. a container that is larger on the inside than on the outside) (2), and others. In the few cases where a score of 2 was identified, the common items were communicating plus a luminous statue (3), communicating plus human plus statue (3). Manifest counterintuition furthermore occurred in 41 cases (67.2%), and the instances where it occurred were based on prompted responses about the qualities of supernatural agents. These reports predominantly referred to omnipotence (37, 60.6%) and in some cases notions of immortality (5), and finally in several cases to seemingly non-counterintuitive standards of moral supremacy (8).

Further, indirect counterintuitive dream content was very common and occurred in 56 analysed reports (91.8%). These were types of representations about which believers might have given counterintuitive descriptions.

These dreams referred to various SA agents, religious sites, objects, and rituals, without explicit markers of counterintuitive properties. Example of indirect counterintuitive dream content can be seen in quotes such as "Shiva/Mahadev appeared and advised me to conduct the puja"; "Durga came and made me wake up. Told me to take a bath."

Counterintuitive representations resemble folk notions about "miracles", or in the Hindu Nepali case, "ajap"/"ascarya". Categorizing a cultural item as a "miracle" might be indicative of counterintuitive content, and highlights religious evaluation. Among 38 informants, 62.3% describe their dream as "ascarya" (a miracle). An allegedly "special" status of the dreams was further recognized among 49 (78.4%) informants who stated that their dream was a ritualized "darshan". Such dream schemata of bilateral perceptual appearance entailed that the dreamer *saw* and had *seen* according to the ritualized principle of "darshan", where redemptive blessings are received through the gaze of a supernatural agent. Informants explicitly identified supernatural dream entities either by "sight" (9, 14.8%), a "feeling" (7, 11.5%), or by "drawing a conclusion" (19, 31%). Interestingly, 33 informants (54.1%) stated that they recognized the supernatural entity through comparison with well-known visual stereotypes of religious images and objects from the cultural environment. For example, one informant dreamt of Vishnu, and was certain that it was Vishnu after comparing the entity with personal experience and prototypes of statues and pictures. Consequently, when informants say they saw "Shiva", the could mean he actually appeared or manifested according to the stereotypical supernatural morphology represented in popular images or statues in the local cultural environment, with the extra attribute of being alive, moving, communicating, and so on.

Summing Up

In this chapter I have used a "piecemeal" or BBA to explore purportedly religious items in the context of supernatural dreaming. The BBA points to the composite (e.g. Svensson, this volume, pp. 82–100) nature of cultural phenomena and can be applied at different levels of abstraction. Consequently, there are building blocks of building blocks. Drawing on some of the many theoretical stances in the cognitive and evolutionary science of religion and anthropology, this chapter has argued that (a) recurrent themes of counterintuitive processing are strong candidates for being building blocks of supernatural dream imagery, (b) supernaturalism is a decisive building block of allegedly religious dreaming; and (c) these dreams are distinct building blocks of purportedly religious experiences and traditions. I have furthermore used, developed, and demonstrated the process of "religious specialness-making" in connection to the BBA (Taves 2011). In particular, I have stressed the way supernaturalism, counterintuition, and high (sacred) values seem to render a kind of affordance-potential (e.g. Gibson 1977) that leads to a further ritualization, theological validation, rationalization and institutionalization connected to the felt specialness of religious dream imagery.

About the Author

Andreas Nordin has a PhD in social anthropology and is an Associate Professor of religious studies and lecturer at the Department of Cultural Sciences, University of Gothenburg, Sweden. Nordin's primary areas of research interest are cognitive and evolutionary anthropology, moral psychology, honour and reputation, religious cognition, and the cognitive science of religion. His recent publications include: "Indirect Reciprocity and Reputation Management in Religious Morality Relating to Concepts of Supernatural Agents," *Journal for the Cognitive Science of Religion* (2015); "Altruism or Mutualism in the Explanation of Honour with Reference to Reputation and Indirect Reciprocity?" *Sociology and Anthropology* (2016); and "Cognition and Transfer of Contagious Substance in Hindu Himalayan Pilgrim Journeys," *Open Theology* (2016).

References

Anttonen, Veikko. 1996. "Rethinking the Sacred: The Notions of 'Human Body' and 'Territory'." In *Conceptualizing Religion: The Sacred and its Scholars: Comparative Methodologies for the Study of Primary Religious Data*, edited by Thomas A. Idinopulos and Edward A. Yonan, 36–54. Leiden: Brill.

Atran, Scott. 2002. *In Gods We Trust: Evolutionary Landscape of Religion*. Oxford: Oxford University Press.

Barnes, Berry S. 1983. "Social Life as Bootstrapped Induction." *Sociology* 17(4): 524–45.

Barrett, Justin L. 2000. "Exploring the Natural Foundations of Religion." *Trends in Cognitive Sciences* 4(1): 29–34.

—2004. *Why Would Anyone Believe in God?* Walnut Creek: Altamira Press.

—2007. "Cognitive Science of Religion: What is It and Why is It?" *Religion Compass* 1(6): 768–86.

—2008. "Coding and Quantifying Counterintuitiveness in Religious Concepts: Theoretical and Methodological Reflections." *Method & Theory in the Study of Religion* 20(4): 308–38.

—2017. "Could We Advance the Science of Religion (Better) without the Concept 'Religion'?" *Religion Brain & Behavior* 7(4): 282–84.

Bloch, Maurice. 2008. "Why Religion is Nothing Special but is Central." *Philosophical Transactions of the Royal Society B: Biological Sciences* 363(1499): 2055–61.

Boyer, Pascal. 2001. *Religion Explained: The Evolutionary Origins of Religious Thought*. New York: Basic Books,

—2005. "A Reductionistic Model of Distinct Modes of Religious Transmission." In *Mind and Religion: Psychological and Cognitive Foundations of Religiosity*, edited by Harvey Whitehouse and Robert N. McCauley, 3–29. Walnut Creek: Altamira Press.

—2013. "Explaining Religious Concepts: Lévi-Strauss the Brilliant and Problematic Ancestor." In *Mental Culture, Classical Social Theory and the Cognitive Science of Religion*, edited by Dimitris Xygalatas and William McCorkle Jr, 164–75. Durham: Acumen Publishing.

Boyer, Pascal, and Charles Ramble, 2001. "Cognitive Templates for Religious Concepts:

Cross-Cultural Evidence for Recall of Counterintuitive Representations." *Cognitive Science* 25(4): 535–64.
Boyer, Pascal, and Michael B. Petersen. 2011. "The Naturalness of (Many) Social Institutions: Evolved Cognition as their Foundation." *Journal of Institutional Economics* 8(1): 1–25.
Brereton, Derek P. 2000. "Dreaming Adaptation, and Consciousness: The Social Mapping Hypothesis." *Ethos* 28(3): 379–409.
Bulkeley, Kelly. 2007. "Sacred Sleep: Scientific Contributions to the Study of Religious Dreaming." In *The New Science of Dreaming: Volume 3, Cultural and Theoretical Perspectives*, edited by Deidre Barrett and Patrick McNamara, 71–94. Westport, CT: Praeger.
—2008. *Dreaming in the World's Religions – a Comparative History*. New York: New York University Press.
—2009. "Mystical Dreaming: Patterns in Form, Content and Meaning." *Dreaming* 19(1): 30–41.
Clark, Andy. 2016. *Surfing Uncertainty: Prediction, Action and the Embodied Mind*. New York: Oxford University Press.
D'Andrade, Roy G. 1961. "Anthropological Studies of Dreams." In *Psychological Anthropology: Approaches to Culture and Personality*, edited by Francis L. K. Hsu, 296–332. Homewood: Dorsey Press.
—2002. "Violence without Honor in the American South." In *Tournaments Of Power – Honor and Revenge in the Contemporary World*, edited by Tor Aase, 61–75. Burlington: Ashgate.
Doniger, Wendy, and Kelly Bulkeley. 1993. "Why Study Dreams? A Religious Studies Perspective." *Dreaming* 3(1): 69–73.
Edgar, Iain R. 2004. "The Dream Will Tell: Militant Muslim Dreaming in the Context of Traditional and Contemporary Islamic Dream Theory and Practice." *Dreaming* 14(1): 21–29.
Gibson, James J. 1977. "The Theory of Affordances." In *Perceiving, Acting, and Knowing: Toward an Ecological Psychology*, edited by Robert Shaw and John D. Bransford, 127–43. Oxford: Lawrence Erlbaum.
Hall, Calvin S., and Robert L. Van de Castle. 1966. *The Content Analysis of Dreams*. New York: Appleton-Century-Croft.
Heintz, Christophe. 2007. "Institutions as Mechanisms of Cultural Evolution: Prospects of the Epidemiological Approach." *Biological Theory* 2(3): 244–49.
Hobson, J. Allen, Edward F. Pace-Schott, Robert Stickgold, and David Kahn. 1998. "To Dream or Not to Dream? Relevant Data from New Neuroimaging and Electrophysiological Studies." *Current Opinion in Neurobiology* 8(2): 239–44.
Howhy, Jacob. 2013. *The Predictive Mind*. New York: Oxford University Press.
Jedrej, Marian Charles, and Rosalind Shaw. 1992. *Dreaming, Religion and Society in Africa*. Leiden: Brill.
Knafo, Ariel, and Tziporit Glick. 2000. "Genesis Dreams: Using a Private, Psychological Event as a Cultural, Political Declaration." *Dreaming* 10(1): 19–30.
Laughlin, Charles D. 2011. *Communing with the Gods – Consciousness, Culture and the Dreaming Brain*. Brisbane: Daily Grail Publishing,
Littlewood, Roland. 2004. "From Elsewhere: Prophetic Visions and Dreams among the People of the Earth." *Dreaming* 14(2-3): 94–106.
Llewellyn, Sue. 2013. "Such Stuff as Dreams are Made on? Elaborative Encoding, the

Ancient Art of Memory, and the Hippocampus." *Behavioral and Brain Sciences* 36(6): 589–607.
—2015. "Dream to Predict? REM Dreaming as Prospective Coding." *Frontiers in Psychology* 6: 1–16.
Lohmann, Roger I. 2003. "Introduction." In *Dream Travelers Sleep Experience and Culture in the Western Pacific*, edited by Roger I. Lohmann, 1–19. New York: Palgrave Macmillan.
Mageo, Jeanette Marie. 2003. *Dreaming and the Self: New Perspectives on Subjectivity, Identity, and Emotion*. Albany, NY: State University of New York Press.
Maquet, Pierre, Jean-Marie Péters, Joël Aerts, Guy Delfiore, Christian Degueldre, André Luxen, and George Franck. 1996. "Functional Neuroanatomy of Human Rapid-Eye-Movement Sleep and Dreaming." *Nature* 12(383): 163–66.
McNamara, Patrick. 2016. *Dreams and Visions – How Religious Ideas Emerge in Sleep and Dreams*. Santa Barbara: Paeger.
McNamara, Patrick, Sanford Auerbach, Patricia Johnson, Erica V. Harris, and Gheorghe D. Doros. 2010. "Impact of REM Sleep on Distortions of Self-Concept, Mood and Memory in Depressed/Anxious Participants." *Journal of Affective Disorder* 122(3): 198–207.
McNamara, Patrick, and Kelley Bulkeley. 2015. "Dreams as a Source of Supernatural Agent Concepts." *Frontiers in Psychology* 19(6): 1–8.
Morinis, Alan E. 1982. "Levels of Culture in Hinduism: A Case Study of Dream Incubation at a Bengali Pilgrimage Centre." *Contributions to Indian Sociology* 16(2): 255–70.
Nordin, Andreas. 2011. "Dreaming in Religion and Pilgrimage: Cognitive, Evolutionary and Cultural Perspectives." *Religion* 41(2): 225–49.
Peluso, Daniela M. 2004. "That which I Dream is True: Dream Narratives in an Amazonian Community." *Dreaming* 14(2-3): 120–235.
Purzycki, Benjamin Grant, and Aiyana K. Willard. 2016. "MCI Theory: A Critical Discussion." *Religion, Brain & Behavior* 6(3): 207–74.
Pyysiäinen, Ilkka. 2001. *How Religion Works: Towards a New Cognitive Science of Religion*. Leiden: Brill.
—2009. *Supernatural Agents: Why We Believe in Souls, Gods, and Buddhas*. Oxford: Oxford University Press.
Renne, Eilsha P. 2004. "Dressing in the Stuff of Dreams: Sacred Dress and Religious Authority in Southwestern Nigeria." *Dreaming* 14(2-3): 120–35.
Revonsuo, Antti. 2000. "The Reinterpretation of Dreams: An Evolutionary Hypothesis of the Function of Dreaming." *Behavioral and Brain Sciences* 23(6): 877–901.
Searle, John. 1995. *The Construction of Social Reality*. New York: Free Press.
—2005. "What is an institution?" *Journal of Institutional Economics* 1(1): 1–22.
Sperber, Dan. 1996. *Explaining Culture: A Naturalistic Approach*. Oxford: Blackwell.
—2017. "Cutting Culture at the Joints?" *Religion Brain & Behavior* 8(4): 42–44.
Sperber, Dan, and Deidre Wilson. 1995. *Relevance Communication and Cognition*. Oxford: Blackwell.
Sørensen, Jesper. 2005. "Religion in Mind: A Review Article of the Cognitive Science of Religion." *Numen* 52(4): 465–94.
—2007. *A Cognitive Theory of Magic*. Lanham, MD: Altamira Press.
Taves, Ann. 2011 [2009]. *Religious Experience Reconsidered: A Building-Block Approach to the Study of Religion and Other Special Things*. Princeton, NJ: Princeton University Press.

Tedlock, Barbara. 1987. *Dreaming: Anthropological and Psychological Interpretations.* Cambridge: Cambridge University Press.
Trompf, Garry W. 1990. *Melanesian Religion.* Cambridge: Cambridge University Press.
Tylor, Edward B. 1871. *Primitive Culture, Volume 2.* London: John Murray.
Valli, Katja, and Antti Revonsuo. 2009. "The Threat Simulation Theory in the Light of Recent Evidence: A Review." *American Journal of Psychology* 122(1): 17–38.

5

Invisible Hands and Sacred Unicorns: Occulture as a Schema for Supernatural Ascriptions in the Millennial Generation

Ingela Visuri

Södertörn University

Cognitive science teaches us that the tendency of reducing complex phenomena saves energy and effort. This is however also what underpins the formation of stereotypes and categorical dichotomies in which one side is privileged over the other (McGarty, Yzerbyt, and Spears 2002). The inclination to think in terms of "good" and "bad" categories of science is – naturally – also found within the study of religions. There are, however, scholars who strive towards conciliation between disciplines, and the endeavour Ann Taves has taken on in bridging the ontological and epistemological divide between the naturalist-oriented psychology of religion and the constructivist-oriented scholars study of religions is a good example of such an aspiration. While most researchers tend to remain within the theoretical and methodological boundaries of the tradition one comprehends better, Taves argues that it is possible to reframe and undercut "the old binary distinction between reductionism and uniqueness" (Taves 2011: 7).

In collaboration with Egil Asprem, Taves is developing models for such work from the interdisciplinary platform of the cognitive science of religion (CSR). Their work departs from the so-called *building block approach* (BBA) (Taves 2013), in which complex cultural concepts (CCCs) such as "magic", "religion", and "esotericism" are *reverse-engineered* (Asprem 2016) and deconstructed into minor elements, rather than operationalizing concepts according to a specific definition. The authors argue that such an approach allows for a non-binary, cross-cultural, and interdisciplinary approach to studying phenomena which otherwise tend to cause divides between scholars: "Focusing on the components that interact to produce events thus allows us to integrate lines of research that are often pursued in disciplinary isolation" (Asprem and Taves 2017: 89).

Another central element is the focus towards emic descriptions. Taves (2011) argues that by paying attention to *attributions* (causal explanations) and *ascriptions* (the characteristics assigned) made by those we study, scholars may spot what people "on the ground" deem as special, sacred, or non-ordinary. In summary, Taves and Asprem encourage scholars from different disciplines to identify various components at play by working bottom-up towards a multi-level model of the phenomena studied.

Heeding to this call, I will in this chapter present an empirical and methodological example of an interdisciplinary study on religious cognition that is much aligned with the BBA. While autism is the focal point of the research project discussed in this chapter, the study also highlights a generational shift in the ascription of non-ordinary powers, which in these millennials[1] appears to depart from occult phenomena in Western popular culture; termed *occulture* by Christopher Partridge (2004–2005). Besides illustrating how emic ascriptions of things set apart from the ordinary may vary between different generations, the chapter also provides a multi-level model of how unusual embodied experiences – which appear to be especially prevalent on the autism spectrum – are understood in terms of occult schemas derived from popular culture.

Participatory Research and Mixed Methods

The study of atypical cognition, such as in autistic individuals, poses specific challenges. There is currently a debate within critical autism studies, in which autistic scholars argue that faulty stereotypes – caused by cognitive autism research – are reinforced by a lack of subjective perspectives from autistic subjects (see McGrath 2017 for an extensive discussion). Such methodological and ethical arguments were taken into consideration when designing this study, and I set out to find a method that would allow for my autistic participants to become actively involved as subjects and partners, and which would support me in bracketing my own expectations.

Another challenge concerned how to find a persuasive form of communication for scholars with differing epistemological, methodological, and theoretical viewpoints, such as the historians of religion, anthropologists, psychologists, cognitive scientists and critical autism researchers that I wanted to engage in dialogue with. The project eventually came to involve mixed methods: questionnaires and psychometric testing were used to provide data that would "speak" to a nomothetically oriented audience

---

1. "Millenials" is the colloquial term for the generation born 1982 and later.

and "photographic interviews" were conducted to capture narratives on religiosity and spirituality from an autistic point of view. These materials were then triangulated (e.g. "put in dialogue"; see Mertens and Hesse-Biber 2012: 78) in order to find joint patterns.

Seventeen young adults (16-21 years old), diagnosed on the high functioning end of the autism spectrum and labelling themselves as "religious" or "spiritual", were recruited in order to capture thick and rich emic descriptions. In line with norms for psychological research, I also put together a non-autistic comparison group, carefully matched regarding gender, age, and views of life to allow for quantitative comparisons between populations.[2] Overturning the traditional preparation of interview questions, each of the autistic participants[3] got a disposable camera and a notebook, and were instructed to prepare their own interviews by taking photos of things (e.g. foods, sounds, experiences, relations, places, objects, ethics) that they deemed as significant for describing their own worldviews.[4]

The material derived from this study can be described in terms of personal "building blocks", and the research process is in many ways aligned with Taves' and Asprem's model for exploring emic ascriptions of things set apart from the ordinary:

> If we want to understand how anything at all, including experience, becomes religious, we need to turn our attention to the processes whereby people sometimes ascribe the special characteristics to things that we (as scholars) associate with terms such as "religious", "magical", "mystical", "spiritual", et cetera. (Taves 2011: 8)

In other words, the participants in this study have provided their personal ascriptions of things and events that they consider to be "religious", "spiritual", "supernatural", "magical", and "non-ordinary". The use of mixed methods has generated an extensive amount of material, and I will therefore zoom in on two findings that illustrate (a) the role of magical narratives, and (b) the process of ascribing supernatural qualities to unusual bodily experiences.

---

2. The comparison group was also formed based on the Autism quotient test (Baron-Cohen *et al.* 2001) to make sure that the cognitive style of participants was not too close to the autism spectrum. One of them was replaced due to high scores.

3. Since qualitative studies are time consuming to conduct and difficult to compare, only the autism group took part in the interviews.

4. Some of the participants chose to use mobile phones or show images from the internet on their laptops instead, and a few who found it difficult to illustrate their narratives visually only prepared notes.

Fantastic Narratives

A rather surprising discovery was how several participants included characters from popular culture in their emic definitions of "spirituality". Catzzy, for instance, brought pictures of her favourite goddess Nocturnal from the computer game *Oblivion*, with whom she interacts in gaming to get better luck:

> I mean, for me I'm spiritual if anything, because I don't believe in that [religious] stuff a lot. At least not quote unquote "real" gods or anything like that, but for me it's more games and stuff I find in movies that is interesting.

She goes on to discuss the *Transformers* universe and the animated movies that depict the fight between two groups of robots: the good Autobots and the evil Deceptacons. Several of these animated and made-up characters have come to life to her, such as the Autobot Jazz, whom Catzzy identifies with for being cheeky and funny, and Optimus Prime whom she describes as wise and safe. When facing problems that need to be solved, she creates inner scenarios in which she interacts with these characters: "I usually make up like a fantasy world but it's like my life, and then I am kind of involved, it's like a mix of the real world and then the Transformers movies".

Andrew similarly describes how he gets absorbed into the magical worlds of the British author J. K. Rowling's book series about the young magician Harry Potter, as well as fantasy novels like *Eragon* and *The Lord of the Rings* (see Visuri 2018), and fantasizes about having his own unicorn or winged horse. For him, the Bible similarly represents a piece of literary work, "it's like another narrative but in our world, but it also feels like a fairy world". This is where he searches for answers about life, and Andrew describes how this commitment has taught him compassion:

> I have realised that showing respect, showing availability, that you can be there for someone, not because you are religious but because it is part of being a human, and that you can try to do things better despite the bad things that have happened before.

These narratives suggest that imaginary worlds and popular characters fill important existential functions and meaning-making processes in the lives of the participants. David, for instance, describes how he "fell in love" during pre-school with the Greek goddess Pallas Athena, identifying with her role as the goddess of wisdom:

> This thing when I was younger and I kind of got bullied, since then I have always been praised for my extreme verbal and intellectual capacity … I've always kind of identified with this geeky four-eyes [laughs] and I mean, she's often described as a safe virgin goddess, but she's also the

goddess of rational war and it's very comforting to have such a protector when you are a child.

When other kids harassed him for being different, he gained strength from his relationship with the goddess. David adds that he has also found strength through "art, music, the creative, and then more from spirituality", which has helped heal this trauma.

Historian of religion Carole Cusack (2019) argues that fantastic narratives, such as Harry Potter, provide one of many alternatives to the institutionally "sacred", and maintains that these are sources for personal meaning-making:

> Since the mid-twentieth century fictional narratives have been used to affirm ultimate concerns for certain people, making fiction fulfil the roles and functions of religious texts. Imaginative practices (such as visual and performing arts, reading and viewing fiction) can provide alternative meaning templates that are now understood by some to meet requirements that were once considered unique to religion. For this to occur, the fictional text must draw upon and reflect human concerns, and afford space for contemplation so individuals can devise or extract personal meaning from the story.

The fantastic and mythical narratives described by the participants fulfil several of Cusack's criteria: they are emotional; feature unprivileged characters striving for a better existence; and involve struggle between good and evil. The narratives are, as Cusack argues, used as springboards into "otherworlds" that transcend everyday reality, which make up platforms for imaginary interaction with the characters. What for others may function as casual entertainment is here described as existentially significant and set apart from the ordinary.

Embodied Supernatural Experience

A second finding regards embodied, sensory experiences that the autistic participants label in terms of supernatural agency, such as sensed presence of spirits, out-of-body experiences, feeling touch, and seeing visions without external input of somatosensory stimuli (see Visuri 2019 for a detailed description). While such experiences occur within the general population, the quantitative data revealed that the autism group scored significantly higher than the comparison group, both regarding (1) how many different types of religious experiences each individual has had (M=4,71; SD=3,69, vs. M=1,94, SD=0.90) and (2) how often each type of experience occurs within the group (e.g. 13 participants in the autism group especially have felt the presence of a spirit, compared to 3 in the comparison group). Embodied experiences were more common among the autistic participants, while the comparison group mostly reported traditional experiences such as prayer responses and feeling the presence of God in a mosque or church.

When analysing the *qualitative* material, such embodied elements were described by 14 of the 17 participants. Anastazia, for instance, describes how spirits in her house make themselves known to her on a daily basis, making books fall out from bookshelves, moving things, and whispering in her ear when she least expects it. Gustav similarly senses the presence of spirits and demons, and describes how he turns to occult reality TV-shows where psychic specialists visit haunted houses, to learn more about such supernatural agency. Sometimes he burns sage to make the more aggressive demons go away, while simultaneously feeling empowered by his ability to sense energies that are hidden to others.

Boyan, who is Muslim, also describes herself as psychic. Just before falling asleep during a trip with her family, she hears frightening sounds from footsteps coming up the stairs towards the room where the family sleeps:

> I didn't have the Quran with me, and [since the non-Muslim parents were also in the room] I couldn't pray to Allah because then I would have to go out of the bedroom to pray but that was where the evil force was.

There are also narratives of physical touch, such as Catzzy feeling a hand on her shoulder when home alone, which she interprets in terms of a visit from a deceased relative.

Several participants describe how they have struggled to grasp such experiences, and how they gradually have developed a magical framework for making sense of potentially frightening incidents (see Visuri 2019). Moreover, a close reading of these narratives reveals that their ascriptions bear a close resemblance to occult descriptions in popular media; a finding which is aligned with scholarly arguments on how magical content is interwoven into everyday lives through fantastic literature, scary movies, computer games, and occult reality-TV (see Partridge 2004-2005; Moberg 2015; Thurfjell 2015). I therefore argue below that this result points to a generational shift in which secular representations of magic are activated in terms of supernatural attributions and interactive, mental partners, much resembling descriptions of religious relations (see Luhrmann 2012).

Discussion

Let us consider how the BBA has contributed to bringing forth the results above. To begin, previous studies on religious cognition in autism have mainly departed from hypotheses testing on ontological *beliefs* (e.g. Norenzayan, Gervais, and Trzesniewski 2012; Gervais 2013; Banerjee and

Bloom 2014; Coleman 2016; Lindeman and Lipsanen 2016; Reddish, Tok, and Kundt 2016; Maij *et al.* 2017), which so far has yielded inconclusive results. When instead departing from emic descriptions, it appears that it is rather *experiences* that are central for these participants, such as the experience of being in relation to a fantastic character, or the sense-making process of unusual sensory experiences.

The results moreover highlight a generational shift in the choice of attributions. The studies mentioned above all draw on *naturalness hypothesis of religion*, which departs from the assumption that beliefs and relations with invisible agents are underpinned by a hypersensitivity to detecting intentionality in the world; a cognitive ability which has supported survival throughout evolution (see, e.g., Barrett 2004). By working bottom-up, it however emerges that a new type of agent is considered significant in this younger, Western, and highly individualized generation. Numerous scholars within the study of Western Esotericism have taken an interest in this phenomenon which Partridge terms *occulture*, but – to the best of my knowledge – this phenomenon has so far been overlooked within the CSR.[5]

Partridge (2004–2005, 2012) argues that esoteric and occult ideas, in the sense of being secretive and hidden, now have become broadly available through a cultural shift in which these concepts are spread by popular media, such as computer games, fantastic literature and horror movies:

> While there are of course occult traditions in organizations that are styled as such, concerned with a sense of gnostic privilege, the culture in which they are embedded is no longer, I would argue, hidden or unfamiliar to most people anymore. It is ordinary, and it is every-day. The well-documented shift from religion to spirituality, the turn to the self, the change of focus from external authority to indirect experience has significantly increased the appeal and respectability of esotericism in the modern world. (Partridge 2012)

The study presented here indeed illustrates how relational and embodied cognition is understood in terms of ideas available in popular culture: Catzzy, for instance, activates an inner dialogue with characters from animated movies in times of crisis, while Boyan draws on an occult

---

5. There are a few publications that relate to cognition and esotericism: Egil Asprem and Markus Altena Davidsen (2017) have co-edited a special issue of *Aries* on "Esotericism and the Cognitive Science of Religion", including an introduction which they both have authored, and an article by Asprem (2017) on kataphatic (imagery-based) practice and predictive coding. There is also the chapter "How to Read Miracle Stories with Cognitive Theory: On Harry Potter, Magic, and Miracle", by István Czachesz (2014). I have, however, not been able to find any CSR-study acknowledging the role of occulture, apart from my own article on sensory supernatural experiences and autistic cognition (Visuri 2019) which draws on the same sample and approach that is discussed in this chapter.

understanding of sounds in a house, which she thinks is haunted by ghosts. While it has often been argued that *cross-cultural* data is crucial to the building of hypotheses in the CSR (e.g. Boyer 1994), the emic descriptions in this study suggest that also collective *cross-generational* appraisals of non-ordinary powers need to be considered. Put differently, there appear to be "cultures within cultures".

Yet another aspect of the BBA is that of reverse-engineering. Taves (2011) argues that the deconstruction of complex cultural concepts allows scholars to connect pre-linguistic forms of experience with discursive practices, and to illustrate such interaction, the findings in this study have been formed into a *multi-level model of unusual sensory experience in autism* (see Fig. 1). The model departs from Armin Geertz's (2010) biocultural theory which is described in neurobiological, cognitive-psychological, sociological, semantic-semiotic levels of reality, and highlights cognition as embrained, embodied, encultured, extended, and distributed.

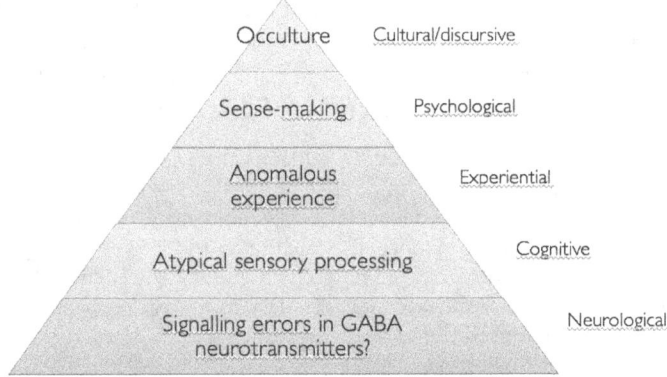

Figure 1: A multi-level model of unusual sensory experience in autism, illustrating the interaction between pre-linguistic and discursive levels of cognition.

The categories in the model are built from an analysis of how the occultured descriptions of reality found in these autistic millenials correspond with the atypical sensory processing found in autism. Beginning with the three bottom levels, autism researchers have suggested that the prevalence of atypical processing of sensory input, which in some cases presents as anomalous perceptual experiences (e.g. feeling touch and seeing visions without external input of sensory stimuli) may be caused by an imbalance in neural excitation and inhibition in GABA neurotransmitters (see Horder *et al.* 2014; Milne, Dickinson, and Smith 2017).

Moving towards the upper levels, the participants describe how such experiences may be confusing, and even terrifying. The attribution of supernatural agency appears to be part of a supportive sense-making process in which they gradually find a means of framing and coping with their experiences: imagining that an invisible touch is caused by a beloved grandmother transforms the sensation into a positive experience, and learning how to deal with evil spirits supports proactive behaviours, such as burning sage or reading the Quran. Occultural narratives come through as central in this discursive process. The model thus illustrates how the experience of atypical sensory processing gradually becomes attributed to non-empirical agents.

A final remark concerns the mixed methods that were applied to enable a conversation with scholars from differing disciplines. While the quantitative measurement highlighted differences between the groups regarding supernatural experiences, the qualitative interviews revealed the role of occulture. Had the design involved only one of these approaches, the interaction between the cognitive and the (oc)cultural framework would have been lost. By applying methods from both naturalist and constructivist frameworks, and by paying attention to the emic categories of the participants, two new findings – that have previously been overlooked – emerged.

Conclusions

The study presented here is an example of how disciplinary boundaries can be bridged methodologically and analytically. By combining a quick, quantitative measure that captured overarching trends in the sample, such as the high prevalence of embodied experiences in autistic subjects, and the slower qualitative process, which elicited narratives on occult ascriptions –the dynamics between cultural input and cognitive underpinnings is elucidated. Put differently: rather than arguing that one discipline is of greater importance than the other, scientific value is added when naturalist and constructivist methodologies are combined.

The study moreover bridges the gap between critical and cognitive autism studies, which draw on differing epistemologies and methodologies. By merging the study of autistic cognition with subjective narratives, and introducing perspectives from the scholarly study of religions, we can connect pre-linguistic dimensions with discursive practices. These connexions have – to the best of my knowledge – not been addressed previously, which may be due to the tendency of staying put within scientific boundaries. Taves and Asprem encourage us to cross such borders, and their BBA has served as a dynamic and useful tool in the uncovering of how these young, Western, autistic participants come to interlace relational and embodied experiences with magical content found in popular media.

About the Author

Ingela Visuri holds a PhD in the study of religions at Södertörn University, Stockholm. Her main work concerns cognitive perspectives on religious behaviours and experiences, which she explores in relation to autistic cognition in her dissertation. Visuri has also published on subjects related to methodological issues, gender and religion, and the didactics of religious education.

References

Asprem, Egil. 2016. "Reverse-Engineering 'Esotericism': How to Prepare a Complex Cultural Concept for the Cognitive Science of Religion." *Religion* 46(2): 158–85.
–2017. "Explaining the Esoteric Imagination: Towards a Theory of Kataphatic Practice." *Aries: Journal for the Study of Western Esotericism* 17(1): 17–50.
Asprem, Egil, and Ann Taves. 2017. "Connecting Events: Experienced, Narrated, and Framed." *Religion, Brain & Behavior* 7(1): 88–93.
Asprem, Egil, and Markus Davidsen, eds. 2017. "Special Issue: Esotericism and the Cognitive Science of Religion." *Aries: Journal for the Study of Western Esotericism* 17(1).
Banerjee, Konika, and Paul Bloom. 2014. "Why Did This Happen to Me? Religious Believers' and Non-Believers' Teleological Reasoning about Life Events." *Cognition* 133(1): 277–303.
Baron-Cohen, Simon, Sally Wheelwright, Richard Skinner, Joanne Martin, and Emma Clubley. 2001. "The Autism-Spectrum Quotient (AQ): Evidence from Asperger Syndrome/High-Functioning Autism, Males and Females, Scientists and Mathematicians." *Journal of Autism and Developmental Disorders* 31(1): 5–17.
Barrett, Justin L. 2004. *Why Would Anyone Believe in God?* Walnut Creek: Altamira.
Boyer, Pascal. 1994. *The Naturalness of Religious Ideas: A Cognitive Theory of Religion*. Berkeley, CA: University of California Press.
Coleman, Thomas. J., III. 2016. *The Social Brain in Human and Religious Evolution: Elucidating the Role of Theory of Mind in (Non)religious Belief*. Chattanooga: University of Tennessee at Chattanooga.
Czachesz, Istvan. 2014. "How to Read Miracle Stories with Cognitive Theory: On Harry Potter, Magic, and Miracle." In *Hermeneutik der frühchristlichen Wundererzählungen: Gesichtliche, literarische und rezeptionsorientierte Perspektiven*, edited by B. Kollmann and R. Zimmermann: 545–58. Tubingen: Mohr Siebeck.
Cusack, Carole M. Forthcoming. "Harry Potter and the Sacred Text: Fiction, Reading and Meaning-Making." In *The Sacred in Fantastic Fandom: Essays on the Intersection of Religion and Pop Culture*, edited by C. M. Cusack, V. L. D. Robertson and J. W. Morehead: 16–32. Jefferson, NC: McFarland.
Geertz, Armin W. 2010. "Brain, Body and Culture: A Biocultural Theory of Religion." *Method and Theory in the Study of Religion* 22(4): 304–21.
Gervais, Will. M. 2013. "Perceiving Minds and Gods: How Mind Perception Enables, Constrains, and is Triggered by Belief in Gods." *Perspectives on Psychological Science* 8(4): 380–94.
Horder, Jamie, C. Ellie Wilson, M. Andreina Mendez, and Declan G. Murphy. 2014. "Autistic Traits and Abnormal Sensory Experiences in Adults." *Journal of Autism and Developmental Disorder* 44(6): 1461–69.

Lindeman, Marjana, and Jari Lipsanen. 2016. "Diverse Cognitive Profiles of Religious Believers and Nonbelievers." *The International Journal for the Psychology of Religion* 26(3): 1–8.

Luhrmann, Tanya M. 2012. *When God Talks Back: Understanding the American Evangelical Relationship with God.* New York: Vintage Books.

Maij, David L. R., Frenk van Harreveld, Will Gervais, Yann Schrag, Christine Mohr, and Michiel van Elk. 2017. "Mentalizing Skills Do Not Differentiate Believers from Non-Believers but Credibility Enhancing Displays Do." *PLoS ONE* 12(8): e0182764.

McGarty, Craig, Vincent I. Yzerbyt, and Russell Spears. 2002. *Stereotypes as Explanations: The Formation of Meaningful Beliefs about Social Groups.* Cambridge: Cambridge University Press.

McGrath, D. James. 2017. *Naming Adult Autism – Culture, Science, Identity.* London: Rowman & Littlefield.

Mertens, Donna M., and Sharlene Hesse-Biber. 2012. "Triangulation and Mixed Methods Research: Provocative Positions." *Journal of Mixed Methods Research* 6(2): 75–79.

Milne, Elisabeth, Abigail Dickinson, and Richard Smith. 2017. "Adults with Autism Spectrum Conditions Experience Increased Levels of Anomalous Perception." *PLoS ONE* 12(5): e0177804.

Moberg, Jessica. 2015. "Hemsökta hus och medielogikens spöken: Spiritualistiska mediers inträde i svensk television under 2000-talet." *Aura: Tidskrift för akademiska studier av nyreligiositet* 7: 5–35.

Norenzayan, Ara, Will M. Gervais, and Kali H. Trzesniewski. 2012. "Mentalizing Deficits Constrain Belief in a Personal God." *PLoS ONE* 7(5): e36880.

Partridge, Christopher H. 2004–2005. *The Re-Enchantment of the West: Alternative Spiritualities, Sacralization, Popular Culture, and Occulture* (Vols. 1–2). London: T&T Clark.

—2012. "Occulture is Ordinary." Keynote speech at Stockholm University, 12 August, 2012. Retrieved from: https://contern.org/online-lectures/christopher-partridge-occulture-is-ordinary/

Reddish, Paul, Penny Tok, and Radek Kundt. 2016. "Religious Cognition and Behaviour in Autism: The Role of Mentalizing." *The International Journal for the Psychology of Religion* 26(2): 1–36.

Taves, Ann. 2011 [2009]. *Religious Experience Reconsidered: A Building-Block Approach to the Study of Religion and Other Special Things.* Princeton, NJ: Princeton University Press.

—2013. "Building Blocks of Sacralities: A New Basis for Comparison across Cultures and Religions." In *Handbook of the Psychology of Religion and Spirituality*, edited by Raymond F. Paloutzian and Crystal Park, 138–61. New York: Guilford Press.

Taves, Ann, and Egil Asprem. 2017. "Experience as Event: Event Cognition and the Study of (Religious) Experience." *Religion, Brain & Behavior* 7: 43–62.

Thurfjell, David. 2015. *Det gudlösa folket: de postkristna svenskarna och religionen.* Stockholm: Molin & Sorgenfrei.

Visuri, Ingela. 2018. "Rethinking Autism, Theism & Atheism: Bodiless Agents and Imaginary Realities." *Archive for the Psychology of Religion* 1: 1–31.

—2019. "Sensory Supernatural Experiences in Autism." *Religion, Brain & Behavior.* https://doi.org/10.1080/2153599X.2018.1548374

6

Qur'ans through the Lens of Moral Foundations: An Explorative Study of Qur'an Translations in a Building Block Framework

Jonas Svensson
Linnaeus University

The "building block approach" (BBA) that Taves and Asprem propose is shared by an increasing number of researchers in the study of religions. The tendency is to break up the "complex cultural concept" of "religion" into parts, and to analyse these parts in turn, without any expectations that they all can be explained in a single manner. This is a way of approaching "religion" academically that I fully support. It provides a means of escaping some of the problems in defining the object of study that haunt the discipline. "Religion" becomes less of a thing "out there" and more of a practical container concept in which to place more tangible cultural phenomena that interest us. It is also, and perhaps even more importantly, as Taves and Aprem note, a way of opening up to cross-disciplinary studies and to participating in the more general, collective academic work towards consilience (Wilson 1998; Slingerland, and Collard 2012).

In my view, the main promise of the move towards consilience, that is, for integrating the sciences and the humanities, is that it allows for a multi-level approach to the study of cultural phenomena as a collective enterprise. Taves' and Aprem's study of religious experience exemplifies this. They choose an approach that could be termed low-level, focused on processes of human perception and appraisal. This is a relevant, even foundational, level. It does not, however, exclude other levels of analysis. It is still possible, and valuable, to approach such experiences in ways perhaps more familiar to most scholars within the humanistic study of religions: for example, describing and categorizing types of experience, investigating correlations between the social position of the experiencer and his/her narratives of that experience, and mapping the intersections between individual narratives and culturally-established narratives, both contemporary and historical.

A BBA can also be applied at different levels. As is the case for non-metaphorical building blocks, the building blocks of cultural phenomena are composite. There are hence building blocks of building blocks. Taves and Asprem give the example of the "theory of mind" as a building block, a basic pan-human "functionally specialized system" (Barrett and Kurzban 2006: 629) in social cognition, central to many existing analyses of religious beliefs and practices (see, e.g., Boyer 2001; Barrett 2004; Bering 2011). This system is itself composite, at least according to one of its "discoverers", psychologist Simon Baron-Cohen. It is made up of smaller building blocks: sets of processes of perception, attention, processing of information, and so on, each of which can, and has been, the focus of dedicated research (Baron-Cohen 1995: 31–58). Moving up a level, the "theory of mind"-system in turn forms a building block of another suggestion for a building block for certain forms of religious thought: the human proclivity for "mind-body dualism" proposed by psychologist Paul Bloom and others (see, e.g., Bloom 2007; Chudek et al. n.d.).

The call for consilience, as I understand it, allows for, and indeed calls for, a multi-level analysis, combined with one particular demand: results at the different levels should not contradict one another. If contradictions emerge, more work is needed to resolve them.

As noted, today there is no lack of suggestions of possible building blocks of religious phenomena. For example, a system of disease avoidance has been suggested as an explanation for certain forms of ritual behaviour (Boyer and Liénard 2006), and a human tendency for costly signalling has been proposed as an explanation for other forms of rituals, as well as religiously framed self-sacrifice (Henrich 2009). Different aspects of memory have been suggested as an explanation for recurring patterns in religious organization and ritual, or "modes of religiosity" (Whitehouse 2004).

A scholar trained in the humanistic study of religion may feel alienated when faced by a BBA. Suggestions for building blocks are often taken from outside of this academic field. Theories have been developed through scientific procedures alien to those trained in textual hermeneutics or ethnographic field work. Here, the notion of consilience can bring some hope. Suggesting building blocks of cultural phenomena is but one step in a scientific process. Suggestions must be approached with cultural data, in large amounts, and of diverse character: historical, textual, and ethnographic. This is where the humanistic study of religions in its traditional forms comes in, both in terms of generating empirical material and in reflecting upon how new discoveries, or suggestions for explanations, relate to results in previous research.

The rest of this chapter is a modest attempt at showing how this might be done. I have chosen a particular theory with a clear building block character and will approach it with a set of data from within my own field of expertise. From this, there may emerge patterns that can be discussed in relation to previous research, but which may also suggest future avenues of scholarly inquiry.

Into the Building Block Quarry: Moral Foundations Theory

The moral foundations theory (MFT) has been developed during the last decade (starting 2004) by psychologist Jonathan Haidt and associates (Haidt 2012; Graham *et al.* 2013). The theory holds that cross-culturally and cross-historically widely diverging cases of third party evaluations of behaviour as "good" or "bad" can be reduced to a set of foundations, or moral intuitions, that in themselves have an origin in human beings as members of an ultrasocial species with evolved psychological biases towards selective non-kin reciprocal altruism. These foundations could hence be seen as a sort of "building blocks" of morality. The original set of foundations is the following:

1. Care. It is morally wrong to harm someone else, at least without legitimate reason (e.g. that the person has violated some other foundation). It is also morally right to help someone else, and care for them.
2. Fairness. It is morally right that everybody (in your group) is treated fairly and in line with a principle of proportionality, in rewards and punishment. It is morally wrong to cheat.
3. Loyalty. It is morally right to be loyal to others belonging to the same group as yourself, and to sacrifice your own well-being for the group. To betray the group to which you belong is morally wrong.
4. Authority. It is morally right to respect whoever is a *legitimate* authority, whether it be a person or an institution. To disobey or subvert legitimate authority is morally wrong.
5. Purity (or Sanctity). Certain things, persons, places, ideas are "sacred", that is, set apart and forbidden, or "pure" and should be treated with respect and reverence and kept clean. Violations of the sacred and defilation of purity are morally wrong.

A sixth foundation has been suggested (and the proponents of MFT are explicitly open to the possibility that there are even more, but probably not fewer): Liberty. It is morally right to let individuals pursue their own interests and it is morally wrong to oppress others or limit their freedom. In the following, however, I will stick to the original list. The main reason for this is that it is in relation to this list that a specific method for analysing texts, which will be applied here, has been developed.

During the time since its emergence, the MFT has received wide interest, and has inspired many empirically-oriented studies. A Google Scholar search on 5 November 2018, for "moral foundations theory" rendered 2210 hits, of which roughly three quarters date from the last four years (2014–). One important area of application has been divisions in American politics. Here, the most notable claimed results are a difference in focus between "Liberals" and "Conservatives", where the former tend to stress more the moral foundations of Care and Fairness than the latter, who are more even in their focus on the five. Hence, the foundations of Authority, Loyalty and Purity tend to be relatively more important to conservatives than they are to liberals (Graham, Haidt, and Nosek 2009; Haidt 2012). The results correlate to some degree with divisions between these groups suggested in previous research (Lakoff 2002). At times, the foundations of Authority, Loyalty, and Purity have been collectively termed as "binding" foundations, related to a hypothesis that they have evolved as psychological proclivities in our species as a result of their effects in strengthening in-group solidary, binding groups together (Graham and Haidt 2010).

Some of the applications of the MFT to date have centred on textual material, utilizing the power of computer-aided text analysis. Such material includes newspaper articles (Sagi and Dehghani 2013; Bowe and Hoewe 2016), tweets (Ji and Raney 2015) and blog posts (Dehghani *et al.* 2014). A common method is word frequency counts, using the Moral Foundation Dictionary, a set of words and word stems associated with each of the above-mentioned foundations. This dictionary was originally created to be used with the software LIWC (Graham, Haidt, and Nosek 2009), in turn developed for text psychometrics (Tausczik and Pennebaker 2010). The dictionary is available from the Moral Foundations homepage (www.moralfoundations.org/othermaterials).

On the homepage, it is claimed that the dictionary can be used "on whatever corpus of text you are interested in". In the following, I take the authors at their word and use the original Moral Foundations Dictionary, without modification, in a computer-aided text analysis (using scripts written in the Python programming language), but on a textual material that falls well within the frame of things "deemed religious" and that to my knowledge has not previously been approached through the lens of the MFT: English translations of the Qur'an. The process consists of two steps. The first is a comparison of the results of the analysis with some suggestions of the MFT. Are there any patterns that arise that are in line with what the theory predicts? If so, there is a second step that can be taken. Can these patterns, in combination with previous (limited) research on Qur'an translations, be used to produce new knowledge concerning these particular texts or alternatively to suggest new avenues for future research?

Some Notes on Materials and Methods

The material consists of a set of dictionaries constructed from 48 English-language Qur'an translations originally published between 1734 and 2018 (see appendix). The dictionaries contain all the words in each translation. Forty-seven of the dictionaries were created, using web scraping, from translations available on the website *islamawakened.com*. One additional dictionary was constructed from a translation available on the website *tanzil.net*. Altogether, these translations represent slightly less than half of the known translations of the Qur'an into the English language (Lawrence 2017). All translations relate to the same basic source text. Almost all are translations from the original Arabic text of the Qur'an, while a few are translations of translations or paraphrases in Urdu or modern standard Arabic. Most of the translations contain words within brackets. These are usually not from the original Arabic text and function at times merely as linguistic clarifications. At times, however, they mirror the translator's interpretations and ideological leanings, which makes them relevant to include in the lexicons when assessing moral foundations in the translations. For example: Muhammad Marmaduke Pickthall's translation of verse 1:3 reads "Thee (alone) we worship; Thee (alone) we ask for help". The word "alone" in is not actually in the Arabic source text. It is an addition that stresses the theological dogma of *tawhid,* or absolute monotheism. As is the case of theological considerations, *moral* considerations can be suspected to hide within brackets in the translations as well.

The Moral Foundations Dictionary was then used to calculate the frequency of the total number of words connected to each foundation to be found in each translation, relative to the total number of words in that translation. The Moral Foundation Dictionary is simply a list of words or word stems. Each word in the list is associated with one (or in a few cases two) foundation(s). The dictionary also differentiates between words related to "virtues" and "vices" within each foundation. The word "betray", for example, is in the list connected to the foundation Loyalty, but as a vice. The word "loyal" is in a separate list, related to the same foundation, but as a virtue. Although I did not make any modifications to the words in the lists, I exchanged the list of words and word stems in the original dictionary for lists of regular expression search patterns. Hence, in searching for terms relating to the word "clean" (associated with the Purity foundation), the search pattern "\sclean\s" searches for the actual word "clean" and nothing else (the part "\s" of the pattern represents a space or new line), while the pattern "\sclean[A-z]+" searches for all words that begin with the word stem "clean" and are followed by any letter until a punctuation mark or a space. In an actual test on all translations, the latter pattern returned the following words: "cleaned", "cleaner", "cleanest", "cleaning", "cleanliness", "cleanly", "cleanness", "cleans", "cleanse", "cleansed", "cleansers", "cleanses", "cleanseth", "cleansing". The same test was done for all patterns constructed. Those patterns that returned obvious false positives were revised or removed. For example: the pattern "\sharm[A-z]+" in the list of words connected to Care/vice returned words such as "harmed" and "harmer", but also the word "harmony", which is not relevant. The pattern was thus changed to "\sharme[A-z]+".

The scores of each foundation (divided into vices and virtues) were stored in a set of ten variables, indicating both the foundation and its orientation. In the following, I will refer to these variables through abbreviations indicating both foundation and orientation. Hence, LP refers to Loyalty/virtue (positive) and LN to Loyalty/vice (negative), AP refers to Authority/virtue, PN refers to Purity/vice, and so on. To clarify: the value of PN for the translation X is the total number of "hits" that the list for PN generates (the total frequency of words deemed to be associated with Purity/vice), divided by the total number of words in X.

Results

It is important to stress what can and cannot be done with this particular method. The results of the frequency analysis cannot be used to ascertain the relative importance of the different foundations *within* one translation. The lists used are of different lengths and are most likely not exhaustive. Hence, it is not possible to say that a particular foundation is more central than another in a particular translation. It is, however, possible to compare translations with one another, that is, whether translations X and Y score differently in relation to foundation F (given the content of the list of that particular foundation).

It is also possible, in this vein, to test for correlations between frequency scores for different translations. The first such correlation study did not return any exciting results. Of a total of 45 possible pairings, eight displayed significant correlations across the 48 translations ($p<,05$). The patterns, however, seemed only partly to be in line with suggestions within MFT. Three of the significant correlations were between the different aspects of Authority and Loyalty (AN-LN, AP-LP, AN-AP) and one between Purity and Authority (PP-AP). At the same time, however, there were unexpected (in relation to the theory) correlations between Loyalty and Care (LP-CN, LN-CN) and between Purity and Fairness (PP-FN).

This test for correlations was done on the raw results from the relative word frequency analysis. When the scores for the whole set of translations were more closely examined, however, it turned out that the distribution around the mean value was positively skewed for all variables except one. In order to adjust for this, I used the log10 method to recalculate the values in all variables but one, in order to better approximate a normal distribution, and ran the correlation study again.

This made a difference. All eight correlations present in the first analysis remained. To this, there were added eight more, resulting in a total of 16 variable pairs with significant correlations out of 45 possible correlations. Now all the variables in the Authority/Loyalty cluster (AP, AN, LP, LN) correlated with one another. Furthermore, three of the variables in this cluster (AN, LN and LP) now correlated with the "vice" aspect of Care, i.e. CN. The correlation between CN and LP displayed the highest correlation of all (r=,54) and the one between CN and LN the third highest (r=,39). The other new correlations that emerged were between FN-LN, FN-AN, CP-AP and CP-AN. PN, PP and FP showed no changes. FP still showed no significant correlation with any of the other variables.

What can be concluded from this? It would appear that at least one suggestion within MFT corresponds with the patterns that protrude. There is a connection between the two "binding" foundations of Loyalty and Authority. They covary at a significant level with one another across translations. Table 1, below, provides the figures (Pearson's *r*):

Table 1: Correlations between foundations Loyalty and Authority

	AP	AN	LP	LN
AP	1	,37	,30	,32
AN	,37	1	,29	,36
LP	,30	,29	1	,28
LN	,32	,36	,28	1

The rest of this chapter concerns what to do with these findings in further explorations.

Moving On

As mentioned above, a recurring application of MFT has been in the context of analysing the role of moral politics in the United States and differences between "liberals" and "conservatives". There, as mentioned above, the two binding foundations that were shown to covary in the set of translations, Authority and Loyalty, also form a cluster (alongside Purity, which, as mentioned above, did not covary with the other two to the same extent in this material) of foundations that are stressed more by conservatives than by liberals.

Now, one can to turn to previous research on Qur'an translations to see whether it has identified any translations as corresponding, at least roughly, to such a distinction between "liberal" and "conservative".

This is not an easy task. More general, academic work on Qur'an translations into English is limited. Several of the relevant works are cited below (however, see also, e.g., Khan 1986; Robinson 1997; Bobzin 2001) Most comparative studies limit themselves to the translation of particular verses, words or idioms (e.g. al-Ghazalli 2012; al-Saggaf, Yasin, and Abdullah 2013; Al Ghamdi 2015) There are, however, in previous research some notes and evaluations of a general character concerning two particular translations present in the set that could be used as a starting point.

The first translation, which, given how it is described in previous research, could be expected to display a "conservative" tendency is the one by Muhammad Taqi ud-din al-Hilali and Muhammad Muhsin Khan first published in 1977. From the mid-1990s, this translation became the translation of choice for the Saudi Arabian worldwide Qur'an distribution machinery (Wild 2015: 173) Religious studies scholar Bruce Lawrence – whose book *The Koran in English* (2017) is one of the more comprehensive comparative studies of English translations – presents it as "highly controversial, yet the most widely distributed Qur'an during the past quarter of a century" (Lawrence 2017: 181). He also notes that it belongs to a set of translations within a "orthodox" tradition representing a "neo-Salafi conservatism" (p. 181). Similar evaluations can be found in other studies (Mohammed 2005; al-Amri 2010: 104; Wild 2015).

On the other hand, English linguistics scholar Abdur Raheem Kidwai, in his book *Translating the Untranslatable* (2011) is full of praise over the translation which he deems to be an "epitome of painstaking scholarship" (Kidwai 2011: 65). From the rest of the book, however, it is clear that Kidwai himself takes on a literalist and highly conservative Sunni position to the activity of translating the Qur'an. One of his harsher judgments is reserved for the translation that I have selected to represent a "liberal" position, which is also one of the few by a female translator: author Laleh Bakhtiar. Kidwai criticizes her for having a mindset influenced by her American context as well as having a "feminist agenda" in her 2007 translation (2011). Lawrence, likewise, but without apparent critique, characterizes the translation as a "feminist rendition of the *Koran* in English" (Lawrence 2017: 100).[1] While "feminist" may not be interchangeable with "liberal", it is perhaps close enough for the purposes of this exploratory investigation, considering also the overall evaluation by translation studies scholar Waleed Bleyhesh al-Amri of the translation as exemplary of a

---

1. For a more detailed analysis of the feminist character of the translation, see Hassen (2011b).

"modernist idiosyncratic approach to tradition and historical method" (al-Amri 2010: 106).

How, then, do these two translations compare with one another, and with the overall mean values of the different variables? And, furthermore, how do the evaluations in previous research on their different character measure up to these results? In order to facilitate this comparison, I normalized all the values using z-scores. This created a unitary measure across the variables in which 0 represents the mean for all translations and 1 and -1 represent a distance of one standard deviation above and below the mean, respectively. Table 2, below, shows the results from the comparison of the two translations in relation to all ten variables as well as the absolute value of the difference between the scores.

Table 2: Comparison between the translations of Bakhtiar and Hilali-Khan, regarding deviation from the mean of all translations.

	AN	AP	CN	CP	FN	FP	LN	LP	PN	PP
Bakhtiar	0,5	-0,6	-2,2	1,5	1,0	-2,0	-1,7	-1,1	-0,3	-0,9
Hilali-Khan	2,0	0,7	0,5	0,0	-0,5	0,5	0,4	-0,9	1,0	0,1
Difference	1,5	1,3	2,7	1,5	1,5	2,5	2,1	0,2	1,3	1,0

From this, it would appear that the suggestion that the two translations are different from one another, based on previous research, holds also when seen through the prism of MFT, apart from the variable LP. It can be noted that of the two, Bakhtiar's translation appears to be the one that stands out most in the set of translations. It deviates from the overall mean with one standard deviation or more on six out of ten possible variables. Hilali-Khan's translation is more in line with the majority, deviating to the same extent on only two variables.

Going Even Further

So far, a Building Block approach, here represented by MFT, has been confronted with the material of Qur'an translations in two ways. Firstly, in checking whether suggestions within MFT have any resonance in these particular texts. The answer here is a cautious, and qualified "Yes". Secondly, existing research on differences in ideological orientation of Qur'an translations was confronted with findings from an application of MFT to the same set. The result from this comparison was again not contradictory, at least. Now it is possible to move on to a more exploratory section where these two findings are combined in order to identify areas in which further reflection in relation to previous research is merited, and new suggestions for future areas of research can be formulated.

While Bakhtiar's and Hilali-Khan's translations are quite different from one another, both are most probably more similar to other translations in the set. Using these two translations as reference points it would be possible to create groups of translations, based on similarities between their scores on at least some of the variables. The test for correlation between variables provided a basis for a selection: AP, AN, LP, and LN. However, I argue that the combined results of the correlation study and the comparison between Bakhtiar's and Hilali-Khan's translations merit the inclusion also of a fifth: CN. This argument is based on a combination of three observations: CN correlates on a significant level with three of the other four variables; its correlations with LP and LN are at a comparably high level; and lastly, it is the variable displaying the highest difference in the comparison between Hilali-Khan's and Bakhtiar's translations.

Settling for these five variables, I used K-means clustering to group translations according to how they score on these variables, setting the preferred number of clusters to six.[2] Three larger and three smaller clusters emerged. Of the three larger, two housed 14 and 15 translations respectively (see appendix). Bakhtiar's translation is present in the first cluster, Hilali-Khan's in the second. Since cluster analysis returns data on the distances between the clusters, it could be concluded that the third largest cluster of ten translations occupied a space in between what will henceforth be referred to as the Bakhtiar and the Hilali-Khan clusters. A word of caution is appropriate: interpreting the results of a cluster analysis is difficult, and theory-dependent. Here, the results are merely used as a starting point for reflection in relation to previous research.

The most striking pattern that emerges is that more than half of the cases (eight) belonging to the Bakhtiar cluster were translations published before the year 1970. Excluding the earliest three translations in the set, that is, three non-Muslim translations published in the eighteenth and nineteenth centuries, all other pre-1970s translations belong to the Bakhtiar cluster.

Possible patterns in the remaining six translations (including Bakhtiar's) are less obvious. Two of them, however, may have ended up in

---

2. K-clustering analysis entails determining the number of clusters beforehand. Determining the appropriate number of clusters is difficult. After testing different options, it turned out that three-four clusters led to the emergence of two major clusters with a large number of translations in each. Five or six clusters generated very similar results with three larger clusters. In all tests (including tests of seven, eight and nine clusters), however, Bakhtiar's and Hilali-Khan's translations ended up in different clusters.

the cluster as a result of a dependence, linguistically, on pre-1970s translations. As I have discussed in an earlier article (Svensson 2019: 220), and has been noted by other commentators, the translation by Hamid Aziz from 2000 is to a large extent a compilation of pre-1970 translations (Lawrence 2017: 184), which could account for its placement in the cluster. Perhaps the same explanation can be given for the 2006 translation of Abu A'la Mawdudi's *tafsir*, which also displays a large lexical overlap with earlier translations (Svensson 2019: 221–22). No direct support for the B cluster being a particularly "liberal" cluster can be found, with one possible exception: It includes the translation by T. B. Irving from 1985. Irving, an American convert, explicitly produced his translation with a modern American audience in mind, indicated by its original subtitle "The first American version". Previous research indicates that this explicit ambition led to some criticism (Greifenhagen 1992: 282).

What then, about the Hilali-Khan cluster? Here, the time aspect is even more striking. No translation in the cluster predates Hilali-Khan's from 1977. The presence of one of the translations within the cluster is explicable in the same way as the case with Aziz's translation above. The translation on *tanzil.net* attributed to a Safi al-Rahman Mubarakpuri turns out, at closer inspection, to be a translation from 2000 of Ibn Kathir's *tafsir* with quotations from the Qur'an to a large extent taken from Hilali-Khan's translation (Amazon.com 2018).

As noted above, previous research places Hilali-Khan's translation in a Salafi ideological context, that is, a context characterized by an ideal of literalism, and puritanism in belief and practice, rejecting any aspects not directly supported by the Qur'an, the Hadith, and the beliefs and practices of the first generations of Muslims. One more translation within the cluster has likewise been characterized in this manner. The so-called *Sahih International*, is a translation from 1997 by three female converts residing in Saudia Arabia. Religious studies scholar Rim Hassen, analysing the translation with a special focus on gender, deems *Sahih International* to be patriarchal in tone. She directly attributes this to the Saudi Arabian context in which it was produced (Hassen 2011a: 227–28). In a 2017 article in the web magazine *The Daily Beast*, reporter Katie Savadski seeks the translators for an interview, after finding that *Sahih International* was the preferred Qur'an translation in much of the English-language propaganda of the Salafi-Jihadi Islamic State in Syria and the Levant (Zavadski 2017).

May then the Hilali-Khan cluster be characterized as cluster of Salafi-oriented translations? The answer is clearly "No". In fact, a large number of translations within the cluster are tied to individuals or groups either explicitly opposed to Salafism, or that are targets of Salafi hostilities. There are at least three translations directly connected to contemporary movements with roots in a Sufi tradition tied to a charismatic leader: the translation by Ali Ünal from 2008, connected to the Turkish Gülen movement (Yavuz 2013); the translation attributed to the Pakistani religious scholar and spiritual leader of the movement *Minhaj ul-Qur'an* Muhammad Tahir-ul-Qadri from 2011; and the translation from 2009 by Indian scholar Wahiduddin Khan, founder and spiritual leader of the *al-Risala movement* (Omar 2006). In the cluster, there is also a translation from 1991 by Amatul Rahman Omar and Abdul Mannan Omar, who are connected to the marginal, and by many Muslims, despised, Ahmadiyya movement, and a Shiite translation by Ali Qara'i from 2004. Perhaps the translation by a certain Bakhtiari Nejad, possibly from 2010, of which I have been unable to retrieve much further information, can also be seen as part of a Shi'a tradition.[3] In any case, there are signs that some view Nejad as an authority; he died in 2010, but there is still a homepage and Facebook page, apparently run by his admirers (last posting in October 2017) featuring his texts and recordings of lectures.

Does the fact that the Hilali-Khan cluster houses both Salafi-oriented translations and translations connected to individuals and groups that could be viewed as representing religious positions different from, and even opposed to, Salafism mean that the method used is flawed? Not necessarily, if one considers the underlying variables for the clustering: that is, (mainly) variables aimed to measure the strength of the *binding* foundations of Authority and Loyalty.

As I have argued elsewhere (Svensson 2012 [2014]; 2015: 143–49) there is an interesting affinity between Salafism and some forms of brotherhood (*tariqa*) Sufism, under the leadership of charismatic figures: the ideal of *deference* to authority. In the Salafi case, it is a matter of deference to the scriptures, and the thought and practice of the first generations of Muslims, the "pious forefathers", in the case of Sufism, deference to the leader, or the wider hierarchy within the group. Deference to the *authority* of the organization and the leader can also be found in the Ahmadiyya case (to the *khalifa* of the movement) and in the Shi'a case (to the clergy, and ultimately to the imams). Connected to this ideal of deference, is the notion that those who defer in these different contexts constitute a group, a group different from those who do not defer, and a group to which *loyalty* is due.

While there are still translations within the cluster that might not fit into this proposed pattern, the fact that half of them do may merit further reflection in relation to previous research that perhaps could shed some light on the more striking pattern of a breaking point in time, in the

---

3. I here rely on a passing reference in Adelkhah (2016: 289), noting that the translation is popular among Afghani Shiites. No source for this information is cited.

1970s.[4] Anthropologist Dale Eickelman and political scientist James Piscatori have suggested that from the 1970s, there has been an intensification of the process of an "objectification" of Islam, namely, a conceptualization among Muslims around the world of the religious traditions as a separate "thing" to be reflected upon and more closely defined in terms of correct beliefs and practices. This change has been affected by larger events and processes, such as the heightened missionary activity connected to Wahhabi ideology financially backed by the Gulf states since the 1970s, the Iranian revolution in 1978/1979 and a general Islamic revival from the 1980s onwards. As a consequence, differences between alternative ways of understanding the tradition, that is, internal divergence, have come to the fore, and become focal points to rally around, and to use as a basis for differentiating between "us" and "them" (Eickelman and Piscatori 2004: 37–45). This raises the question whether acts of Qur'an translation could be seen as part of an intra-Muslim "battle for souls", and whether differences detected here between the Bakhtiari and the Hilali-Khan clusters mirror increasing tension and polarization between groups.

Discussion

The aim of this chapter has been to show how a BBA, here exemplified by the MFT, can be applied to a form of material that many scholars in the study of religions are familiar with and have a competence to analyse and reflect upon in a scholarly way. The MFT is but one among many proposals, more often than not formulated outside of the field of the study of religions proper, that complex cultural phenomena can be reduced to a set of basic building blocks, at different levels of complexity. My suggestion is that instead of rejecting such proposals off-hand as "reductionist" or "scientist", and alien to a humanistic tradition of interpretation rather than explanation, we as scholars in the study of religions should engage with them, and confront them with the data we know best, and with results arrived at through traditional or new methods of humanistic scholarship. Who knows, in the end it may turn out that what initially appear to be totally different, even irreconcilable ways to academically approach human culture, are merely scholarship on different levels, which are possible to combine in a shared, and collective aspiration towards consilience.

---

4. I double-checked for this pattern through a comparison of means on the different variables between translations published before and after 1970 (independent samples T-test). The result was that three variables showed significantly different means, all of them used in the cluster analysis: AN, LP, and CN.

About the Author

Jonas Svensson is a Professor in the study of religions at Linnaeus university. He specializes in Islamic studies, and has of late taken a particular interest in integrating the cognitive science of religion into his research field, as well as in ways in which to utilize computers and programming in humanistic research.

References

Adelkhah, Fariba. 2016. *The Thousand and One Borders of Iran: Travel and Identity*. London: Routledge.
Amazon.com. 2018. *The Qur'an & Tafsir Ibn Kathir: Part 1*. https://www.amazon.com/Quran-Tafsir-Ibn-Kathir-Part/dp/B00D0EC8KI (accessed October 1, 2018).
al-Amri, Waleed Bleyhesh. 2010. "Qur'ān Translation and Commentary: An Unchartered Relationship?" *Islam & Science* 8(2): 81–110.
Al-Saggaf, Mohammad Ali, Mohamad Subakir Mohd Yasin, and Imran Ho Abdullah. 2013. "Cognitive Meanings in Selected English Translated Texts of the Noble Qur'an." *QURANICA-International Journal of Quranic Research* 4(1): 1–18.
Baron-Cohen, Simon. 1995. *Mindblindness: An Essay on Autism and Theory of Mind*. Cambridge: MIT Press.
Barrett, H. Clark, and Robert Kurzban. 2006. "Modularity in Cognition: Framing the Debate." *Psychological Review* 113(3): 628–47.
Barrett, Justin L. 2004. *Why Would Anyone Believe in God?* Walnut Creek: AltaMira Press.
Bering, Jesse. 2011. *The Belief Instinct: The Psychology of Souls, Destiny, and the Meaning of Life*. New York: W. W. Norton.
Bloom, Paul. 2007. "Religion is Natural." *Developmental Science* 10(1): 147–51.
Bobzin, Harmut. 2001. "Translations of the Qur'an." In *Encyclopaedia of the Qur'an*, edited by Jane Dammen McAuliffe, [on-line edition, n.p.]. Leiden: Brill.
Bowe, Brian J., and Jennifer Hoewe. 2016. "Night and Day: An Illustration of Framing and Moral Foundations in the Oklahoma Shariah Amendment Campaign." *Journalism & Mass Communication Quarterly* 93(4): 967–85.
Boyer, Pascal. 2001. *Religion Explained: The Human Instincts that Fashion Gods, Spirits and Ancestors*. London: Vintage.
Boyer, Pascal, and Pierre Liénard. 2006. "Why Ritualized Behavior? Precaution Systems and Action Parsing in Developmental, Pathological and Cultural Rituals." *Behavioral and Brain Sciences* 29: 1–56.
Chudek, Maciek, Rita McNamara, Susan Burch, Paul Bloom, and Joseph Henrich. n.d. "Developmental and Cross-cultural Evidence for Intuitive Dualism." Unpublished manuscript. Available from http://www2.psych.ubc.ca/~henrich/pdfs/ChudekEtAl_InutiveDualism_WorkingPaper_June2014.pdf
Dehghani, Morteza, Kenji Sagae, Sonya Sachdeva, and Jonathan Gratch. 2014. "Analyzing Political Rhetoric in Conservative and Liberal Weblogs Related to the Construction of the 'Ground Zero Mosque'." *Journal of Information Technology & Politics* 11(1): 1–14.
Eickelman, Dale F., and James P. Piscatori. 2004. *Muslim Politics*. Princeton, NJ: Princeton University Press.

Al Ghamdi, Saleh A. S. 2015. "Critical and Comparative Evaluation of the English Translations of the Near-Synonymous Divine Names in the Quran." PhD dissertation, University of Leeds.

Al-Ghazalli, Mehdi F. 2012. "A Study of the English Translations of the Qur'anic Verb Phrase: The Derivatives of the Triliteral." *Theory and Practice in Language Studies* 2(3): 605–12.

Graham, Jesse, and Jonathan Haidt. 2010. "Beyond Beliefs: Religions Bind Individuals into Moral Communities." *Personality and Social Psychology Review* 14(1): 140–50.

Graham, Jesse, Jonathan Haidt, Sena Koleva, Matt Motyl, Ravi Iyer, Sean P. Wojcik, and Peter H. Ditto. 2013. "Moral Foundations Theory: The Pragmatic Validity of Moral Pluralism." *Advances in Experimental Social Psychology* 47: 55–130.

Graham, Jesse, Jonathan Haidt, and Brian A. Nosek. 2009. "Liberals and Conservatives Rely on Different Sets of Moral Foundations." *Journal of Personality and Social Psychology* 96(5): 1029–46.

Greifenhagen, Franz V. 1992. "Traduttore Traditore: An Analysis of the History of English Translations of the Qur'an." *Islam and Christian-Muslim Relations* 3(2): 274–91.

Haidt, Jonathan. 2012. *The Righteous Mind: Why Good People are Divided by Politics and Religion*. London: Allen Lane.

Hassen, Rim. 2011a. "English Translation of the Quran by Women: The Challenges of 'Gender Balance' in and through Language." *MonTi* 3: 211–30.

—2011b. "Feminist Translation Strategies and the Quran: A Study of Laleh Bakhtiar's Translation." In *Interfacing Disciplines: Textual Narratives of Departure, Navigation and Discovery*, edited by Rim Hassen and Susan Bassnett, 25–36. Coventry: University of Warwick.

Henrich, Joseph. 2009. "The Evolution of Costly Displays, Cooperation and Religion: Credibility Enhancing Displays and their Implications for Cultural Evolution." *Evolution and Human Behavior* 30(4): 244–60.

Ji, Qihao, and Arthur A. Raney. 2015. "Morally Judging Entertainment: A Case Study of Live Tweeting during Downton Abbey." *Media Psychology* 18(2): 221–42.

Khan, Mofakhkhar Hussain. 1986. "English Translations of the Holy Qur'an: A Bio-bibliographic Study." *Islamic Quarterly* 30(2): 82–107.

Kidwai, Abdur Raheem. 2011. *Translating the Untranslatable: A Critical Guide to 60 English Translations of the Quran*. New Dehli: Sarup Book Publishers.

Lakoff, George. 2002. *Moral Politics: How Liberals and Conservatives Think*. Chicago: University of Chicago Press.

Lawrence, Bruce B. 2017. *The Koran in English*. Princeton, NJ: Princeton University Press.

Mohammed, Khaleel. 2005. "Assessing English Translations of the Qur'an." *The Middle East Quarterly* (Spring): 58–71.

Omar, Irfan. 2006. "Islamic Thought in Contemporary India: The Impact of Mawlana Wahiddudin Khan's al-Risala Movement." In *The Blackwell Companion to Contemporary Islamic Thought*, edited by Ibrahim M. Abu-Rabi', 75–87. Oxford: Blackwell.

Robinson, Neal. 1997. "Sectarian and Ideological Bias in Muslim Translations of the Qur'an." *Islam and Christian-Muslim Relations* 8(3): 261–78.

Sagi, Eyal, and Morteza Dehghani. 2013. "Measuring Moral Rhetoric in Text." *Social Science Computer Review* 32(2): 132–44.

Slingerland, Edward G., and Mark Collard. 2012. *Creating Consilience: Integrating the Sciences and the Humanities*. New York: Oxford University Press.

Svensson, Jonas. 2014. "Mind the Beard! Deference, Purity and Ritualisation of Everyday Life as Micro-factors in a Salafi Cultural Epidemiology." *Comparative Islamic Studies* 8(1-2): 185–209.
—2015. *Människans Muhammed*. Stockholm: Molin & Sorgenfrei.
—2019. "Computing Qur'ans: A Suggestion for a Digital Humanities Approach to the Question of Interrelations between English Qur'an Translations." *Islam and Christian-Muslim Relations* 30(2): 211–29.
Tausczik, Yla R, and James W. Pennebaker. 2010. "The Psychological Meaning of Words: LIWC and Computerized Text Analysis Methods." *Journal of Language and Social Psychology* 29(1): 24–54.
Whitehouse, Harvey. 2004. *Modes of Religiosity: A Cognitive Theory of Religious Transmission, Cognitive Science of Religion Series*. Walnut Creek: AltaMira Press.
Wild, Stefan. 2015. "Muslim Translators and Translations of the Qur'an into English." *Journal of Qur'anic Studies* 17(3): 158–82.
Wilson, Edward O. 1998. *Consilience: The Unity of Knowledge*. London: Little, Brown.
Yavuz, M. Hakan. 2013. *Toward an Islamic Enlightenment: The Gülen Movement*. Oxford: Oxford University Press.
Zavadski, Katie. 2017. "How Three American Women Translated One of the World's Most Popular Qurans." *The Daily Beast*, 2017-03-26.

Appendix:
List of Translations Used and Some Cautionary Notes

As mentioned above, the main website used here for constructing the dictionaries is *islamawakened.org*. It is but one of several websites featuring various translations of the Qur'an, but the most comprehensive (see Lawrence 2017: 93). The administrators have collected translations found elsewhere and include also what they term as "controversial" translations. *Tqnzil.net* has been used in one case, with the only translation not found on *islamawakened.org*. This website has a similar character as *islamawakened* but is less comprehensive.

Dates given in the appendix are questionable. I have used what information that I have been able to collect. In cases where the date is given on the websites, this has been used. In other cases, I have used information retrieved elsewhere on the year of publication of the first translation. There is no guarantee that the texts of the online versions are identical to texts of the first editions. Revised editions may have been used to in the construction of the digital version. For those translations where information on the original year of publication is ambiguous, I have used what I judge to be the most likely information but indicated uncertainty with a question mark. It should be noted that there is no guarantee that the digital versions used in this chapter actually correspond to any published works. To verify this would be a difficult task. For the main purpose of this article, however, that concerns method, this is of lesser importance. The results reached, however, must be interpreted with this in mind.

The list also indicates the placement of translations in either the Bakhtiar (B) or the Hilali-Khan (HK) clusters.

George Sale	*The Koran* (1734)
John Rodwell	*The Koran* (1861
Edward Palmer	*The Qur'an* (1880).
Muhammad Ali,	*The Holy Qur'an* (1917) (B)
Muhammad M. Pickthall	*The Meaning of the Glorious Koran* (1930) (B)
Abdallah Yusuf Ali	*The Holy Qur'an* (1938) (B)
Arthur J. Arberry	*The Koran Interpreted* (1955) (B)
Sher Ali	*The Holy Qur'an* (1955) (B)
N. J. Dawood	*The Koran* (1956) (B)
Abdul-Majid Daryabadi	*The Holy Qur'an* (1957) (B)
M. H. Shakir	*The Qur'an* (1968) (B)
Muhammad Muhsin Khan; Muhammad Taqi ud-din al-Hilali	*Interpretation of the Meanings of the Noble Qur'an* (1977) (HK)
Muhammad Asad	*The Message of the Qur'an* (1980)
Abu-Shabanah; Abdel Khalek Himmat	*Al- Muntakhab [The Select]* (c. 1980) (HK)
Rashad Khalifa	*Qur'an* (1981)
Muhammad Sarwar	*The Holy Qur'an* (1982)
Ahmed Ali	*Al-Qur'an: A Contemporary Translation* (1984[?]) (HK)
T. B. Irving	*The Qur'an* (1985) (B)
Faridul Haque (transl. of Reza Khan Barelvi	*Kanzul Iman) The Holy Qur'an* (1988) (B)
Amatul Rahman Omar and Abdul M. Omar	*The Holy Qur'an* (1991) (HK)
Mohamad Ahmed; Samira Ahmed	*The Koran* (1994)

Mahmoud Ghali	Towards Understanding the Ever-Glorious Qur'an (1997[?]) (B)
Muhammad Farooq-i Azam Malik, *Al-Qur'an* (1997)	
Amatullah J. Bantley; Umm Muhammad; Aminah Assami	The Qur'an [Sahih International] (1997) (HK)
Syed Vickar Ahamed	The Glorious Qur'an (1999) (HK)
Abdalhaqq Bewley; Aisha Bewley	The Noble Qur'an (1999)
Safi ar-Rahman al-Mubarakpuri	Tafsir Ibn Kathir (2000) (HK)
Hamid S. Aziz	The Meaning of the Holy Qur'an with Explanatory Notes (2000) (B)
Hasan Qaribullah; Ahmad Darwish	The Meaning of the Glorious Qur'an (2001)
Kamal Omar	Al-Kitab (2002) (HK)
Shabbir Ahmed	The Qur'an as It Explains Itself (2003)
Ali Quli Qara'I	The Qur'an with a Phrase by Phrase English Translation (2004[?]) (HK)
Abdel Haleem	The Qur'an (2004)
Bijan Moeinian	An Easy to Understand Translation of the Qur'an (2005) (HK)
Zafar Ishaq Ansari (transl. of Abu A'la Maududi)	Towards Understanding the Qur'an (2006) (B)
Laleh Bakhtiar	The Sublime Qur'an (2007) (B)
Taqi Usmani	Ma'ariful Qur'an (2007)
Ali Ünal	The Qur'an with Annotated Interpretation in Modern English (2008) (H-K)
Wahiduddin Khan	The Qur'an (2009) (HK)
Talal A. Itani	Qur'an in English (2009)

Bakhtiari Nejad	*Quran Asan* (2010[?]) (HK)
The Monotheist Group	*The Message* (2011)
Munir Munshey	*The Entire Noble Quran* (2011[?])
Mohammad Tahir-ul-Qadri	*Irfan-ul-Quran (Translation of the Holy Quran)* (2011[?])(HK)
Safi Kaskas	*The Last Testament/The Qur'an* (2015)
Mustafa Khattab	*The Clear Qur'an* (2015) (HK)
A. L. Bilal Muhammad *et al.*	*Quran* (2017)
Mohammad Shafi	*Qur'aanic Studies* (2018)

7

Computing Consilience:
How Modelling and Simulation can Contribute to Worldview Studies

F. LeRon Shults

University of Agder, Kristiansand

Introduction

The Building Block Approach (BBA) championed by Ann Taves and Egil Asprem aims to provide a method for analysing and explaining "complex cultural phenomena in terms of the constituent parts that interact to produce them" (p. 5). Their proposal has many constituent parts that interact to produce the BBA itself, each deserving further analysis and explanation. It was tempting to use this opportunity to highlight their concern about the term "religion" and their recommendation of the term "worldview", but I have made it clear elsewhere that I share these concerns and endorse this recommendation (Shults 2018; Shults, Gore, Lemos, *et al.* 2018). In this context, I decided to focus instead on the second main problem the BBA was designed to solve – achieving consilience – and the role that reverse engineering and predictive processing are supposed to play in fulfilling that transdisciplinary task.

That is a lot to discuss in one chapter. And so I further limit myself by focusing on the extent to which these particular constituent parts of the BBA can be facilitated by the use of conceptual practices and technological tools within the field of computer modelling and simulation (CMS). As the title of my chapter suggests, my overarching goal is to explain some of the ways in which CMS can contribute to the proposed task of constructing epistemological bridges across the sciences and the humanities. This becomes explicit in the fourth main section below. As steps on the way to that goal, sections two and three argue for the usefulness of CMS methodologies for advancing the research strategy at the heart of the BBA (reverse engineering) and for clarifying the evolved bio-cognitive dynamics which Taves and Asprem suspect are at the heart of human worldview construction and maintenance (predictive processing). First, however, I need to say a bit more about the methodological innovations whose virtues I am extolling.

Computer Modelling and Simulation

Especially for those more comfortable with qualitative or hermeneutical methods, CMS may initially seem quite alien. Keep in mind, however, that the way humans naturally keep things in mind is through modelling and simulation. That is to say, mental models of phenomena emerge somewhat spontaneously and simulations of alternative scenarios play out rather regularly in our heads. This is (hopefully) happening in the imagination of the reader right now. What are the relationships among the constituent parts of BBA? Where is the author going with this line of thought? You will have to keep reading to find out, but my preliminary point here is that computational methods enable us to extend our natural human capacities: now we can model far more complex systems and simulate the dynamic interactions among their variable components far more quickly, efficiently, and accurately.

CMS has been utilized in the natural sciences since the middle of the last century and since then has been increasingly adopted by analysts in governments, businesses, and other organizations faced with understanding and predicting complex adaptive systems (Miller 2007; Tolk 2012; Hamill and Gilbert 2015). Interest in CMS techniques among social scientists has grown rapidly in the new millennium, as scholars in fields such as social psychology and sociology have discovered that computational methods provide new ways of exploring the interactions among micro- and macro-level factors that shape human emotions, norms, and institutions (Conte, Andrighetto and Campennì 2014; Gratch and Marsella 2014; Hauke, Lorscheid and Meyer 2017). In recent years these tools have also been gradually capturing the interest of scholars in the humanities who can use them to construct artificial societies within which they can test their theories about human agents and cultures (Dignum and Dignum 2014; Youngman and Hadzikadic 2014; Wildman, Fishwick, and Shults 2017).

CMS has had such a profound effect on such a diversity of academic disciplines that it has been called the "third pillar" of science, alongside theory and experimentation (Benioff and Lazowska 2005; Tolk 2015). What's the big deal? These methodologies require researchers to surface and formalize their assumptions and conceptions with enough precision that the postulated causal interactions among variables can be quantified within algorithms that structure computational architectures and drive exploratory simulations of the relevant multi-dimensional parameter space of a model. In addition to fostering conceptual clarity, CMS also enables us to "experiment" on artificial agents and societies in ways that would not be feasible (or allowed by an internal review board) in the real world. Insofar as a computational model can be appropriately verified and validated (through time-tested techniques) in relation to empirical data from other research methods, results from simulation experiments on the behaviour of its state space over time can shed light on the actual mechanisms at work in the target phenomena.

But do we have any reasons for being optimistic that any of this could be relevant for bolstering BBA and the practice of worldview studies? Asprem and Taves think so. In the context of defending their proposal for incorporating "explanation" into the study of religion within the humanities, they argue that computer modelling and simulation could facilitate the testing of hypotheses and the refinement of historical theories at a much more sophisticated level (Asprem and Taves 2018b: 198). This confidence is warranted, in part, by Taves' own experience (in collaboration with the author of this chapter and other members of the Modelling Religion Project) as a subject matter expert in the construction of a computational model of Rodney Stark's theory of new religious movements (Taves 2019a). Taves' sanguinity toward CMS is also reflected in her appreciative statements in response to Justin Lane's proposal for testing her hypotheses about "revelatory events" through the construction of a computational model (Lane 2018; Taves 2019b).

Another reason to be initially hopeful about the capacity of CMS to contribute to the BBA in general and to worldview studies in particular is the successful development in recent years of several computational models that have shed light on the psychological and social factors at work in the (trans)formation of more or less "religious" worldviews, including the transmission of religious violence in the Radical Reformation (Matthews et al. 2013), the role of cooperation style and contagious altruism in proselytizing religions (Roitto 2015), the function of priestly elites in the emergence of large-scale cooperative societies (Dávid-Barrett and Carney 2015), and the impact of mortality salience on beliefs and behaviours related to supernatural agents (Shults, Lane, et al. 2018). The remainder of this chapter is an attempt to provide even more warrant for this optimism.

Reverse Engineering

The "first step" in the BBA, as Taves and Asprem make clear in their introductory essay for this volume, is reverse engineering, a process which they unpack in light of the "new mechanism" in the philosophy of science. Many humanists might raise their eyebrows at the idea of incorporating engineering of any sort into their work, and balk at the suggestion that their disciplines should aim for "mechanistic" (or any other) kinds of "explanation". Yet this is the medicine Taves and Asprem prescribe for healing the unfortunate divide between those who study religion – and other complex cultural concepts (CCCs) – within fields such as cognitive science and evolutionary psychology, on the one hand, and those who approach such phenomena from a humanist perspective as historians or "religious studies" scholars, on the other. Although this naturalist medicine might feel particularly repugnant to constructivists, the pill is not as bitter as it might seem.

Unlike early modern mechanistic philosophy, which searched for universal and fundamental physical causes, the new mechanism explores local interactions among entities (or forces) and, because it is grounded in evolutionary biology, its explanations are also meant to apply to goal-oriented or intentional behaviours. In the words of William Bechtel (2009), one of the leading proponents of the new mechanism, the latter is meant to foster robust explanations of complex phenomenon by trying to make sense of the relevant mechanisms not only by a reductive "looking down" to identify the component parts, but also by "looking around" at the way in which they are organized and "looking up" at the situation in which they are embedded.

As Asprem and Taves point out in their proposal for incorporating this kind of "explanation" into the study of religion and other CCCs, in this view mechanisms "can be conceived vertically as nested levels of mechanisms and horizontally in terms of causal chains distributed along spatiotemporal lines" (2018a: 12). Both authors, writing individually, go out of their way to emphasize that reverse engineering is not simply about breaking things down through reduction – it is also about *reconstruction*. Taves insists that "to build effective bridges between the historical and the scientific study of religion we not only need to break religion down into its parts but also to test to see if the parts can be reassembled into wholes" (Taves 2015: 192). And in his reverse engineering of the CCC "esotericism", Asprem emphasizes that the BBA is neither essentialism nor reductionism but a process that aims "to reconstitute the objects of study through *vertical* and *horizontal integration*" (Asprem 2016: 22).

So, in what sense is CMS relevant for this "first step" in the BBA? In fact, reverse engineering is at the core of several of the most popular techniques in this field. In the construction of multi-agent artificial intelligence models, for example, the process typically begins by attempting to identify some of the key mechanisms at work in the production of the emergent dynamics of the target phenomenon (looking down). However, making sense of these dynamics requires attending to the way in which the component parts are organized and the behavioural rules that guide their interaction (looking around). Moreover, the interaction of the parts may differ significantly under various conditions, and so computer engineers and subject matter experts must jointly decide on which parameters or social network effects must be included and varied in the environment of the artificial society (looking up).

Let me offer a concrete example. Our research team recently published a generative model of the mutual escalation of anxiety between religious groups (Shults, Gore, Wildman, et al. 2018). Two of the key individual variables of the simulated agents in this model were the tendency to appeal to supernatural agency when trying to explain ambiguous or frightening phenomena and the tendency to appeal to supernatural authorities when trying to defend in-group behavioural norms. We referred to these tendencies as anthropomorphic promiscuity (AP) and sociographic prudery (SP) respectively. Although each of these tendencies could be (and have been) further reverse engineered (see Shults 2015, 2018), they represent an initial fractionation of individual behaviours that are often deemed "religious". In other words, we began by "looking down" at some of the key mechanisms – in this case naturally evolved cognitive and coalitional biases – that empirical research suggests play a role in shared imaginative engagement with supernatural agents (or, to use the more popular complex cultural concept, religion).

However, we also "looked around" at the way in which these biases could be differentially organized and operate differently in relation to other relevant factors (such as mortality salience, social identity, and identity fusion). These latter factors can impact the way in which AP and SP (and their constituent parts) are expressed as human minds organize themselves in human groups. Moreover, contextual, cultural and environmental variations in the environments also impact the way in which religious tendencies are manifested in human populations, and so we also "looked up" at the environmental parameters that shape the situations within which these biases are expressed (or contested). Simulation experiments on the model were able to identify some of the conditions under which – and the mechanisms by which – xenophobic anxiety between religious groups emerges and escalates. In this way, we were able to reverse engineer (and reconstruct) the phenomenon of religious intergroup conflict in an artificial society.

Predictive Processing

As noted above, for Taves and Asprem the place to start in the BBA is with reverse engineering and the place to start in understanding human cognition is with predictive processing. The latter, as they emphasize in their introductory essay for this volume, is "the most fundamental building block" of worldviews and ways of life. Predictive processing is "a computation-like modelling process which approximates Bayesian inferences and which is thought to be central to cognition as well as to natural selection itself" (p. 20). Elsewhere they spell out the rationale for these claims in light of the hierarchical predictive coding (HPC) framework in which top-down predictions interact with bottom-up signals (error monitoring) as an organism continuously evaluates and makes new inferences based on its experience of stimuli in the environment (Asprem and Taves 2017; Taves and Asprem 2017). The basic idea here is that human cognition (and indeed all cognition) is an inherently predictive process, which implies that an adequate explanation of the former will include a clear model of the latter.

What does this have to do with CMS? First, techniques in this field have already been used to construct a wide variety of computational architectures designed to simulate human cognition. Many of these incorporate the sort of differentiated mechanisms that are of interest to scholars of predictive processing. One of the most well-known is the CLARION cognitive architecture, which integrates modules for implicit and explicit action-centred knowledge, using back propagation algorithms to simulate the development of implicit skills at the "bottom level" and extraction algorithms to simulate the identification and selection of rules at the "top level" (Sun 2001; see also Sun and Mathews 2012). As CMS methodologies grow in popularity in the study of "religious" cognition, we will be able to construct cognitive architectures that explicitly simulate predictive and other relevant processes (Shults 2019c).

Second, many computational models are explicitly designed to enable simulation experiments that are capable of predicting the behaviour of the model which, in turn, is supposed to provide insight into the way some mechanisms in the real world may behave in the future (under alternative parametric conditions). Although it is a somewhat contentious term with a variety of meanings (Hassan et al. 2013), most CMS practitioners, like most other scientists, agree that the capacity to "predict" (in some sense) is an appropriate and even central goal in their scientific work. Insofar as CMS continues to offer new insights into – and to extend our capacity for – predictive processing, it can be of significant use in the refinement of the BBA in general and development of "worldview studies" in particular.

For example, another computational model recently published by our research team was able to predict the (real world) shifts in religious variables in 22 countries up to three times more accurately than linear regression analysis (Gore et al. 2018). This model was calibrated and validated using data from the International Social Survey Programme and the Human Development Index. Its simulated agents followed interaction rules based on social influence theories of educational homophily. Simulation experiments showed that the extent to which agents' religious practices, belief in supernatural agents, and belief in God, increased or decreased was strongly influenced by the educational level of their social networks and sense of existential security. The emergence of macro-level shifts in (non)religiosity in the population of the artificial society, which was not programmed into the algorithms guiding the micro-level agent interactions, lends plausibility to arguments (based on other empirical research) that education and existential security are mechanisms that lower religiosity at the population level.

Achieving Consilience

In the Introduction I indicated that the overarching purpose of this chapter is to highlight the potential role of CMS for contributing to the second main task for which Taves and Asprem developed the BBA: achieving consilience between naturalists and constructivists in general, and especially between scholars who study CCCs such as religion from distinctive scientific and humanistic perspectives. The previous two sections pointed to some of the ways in which CMS techniques can facilitate the clarification (and practice) of reverse engineering and the explanation (and enhancement) of predictive processing, sub-tasks which are at the heart of their proposal. In this final section, I address more explicitly some of the ways in which these methodologies can foster the creation of consilience and inform the construction of worldview studies.

I briefly alluded above to the fact that computational tools such as multi-agent artificial intelligence models allow researchers to study the relationships between micro- and macro-level variables in a way that has never before been possible. A well-constructed and well-validated model can generate or "grow" population level phenomena from individual level interactions, shedding light on bottom-up causal mechanisms. It can also shed light on the top-down constraining influence of environmental parameters on the behaviours of simulated agents in an artificial society. Insofar as the computational architectures of such models incorporate insights from disciplines that focus on different levels of analysis, they can be seen as complex theoretical syntheses themselves. The model of mutually escalating religious xenophobic anxiety mentioned above, for example, integrated a variety of theories that attend to both micro- and macro-level variables, including terror management theory, social identity theory, and identity fusion theory.

A different sort of transdisciplinary theoretical integration is possible with system-dynamics models (SDMs). Instead of representing agents and their interactions, such models can express the flow of some quantity between stocks, with the relationship between stocks and rates of flow being determined by differential equations. For example, we developed an SDM of the flow of people from hunter-gatherer to sedentary-agriculturalist lifestyles (or *ways of life*) in which the flow was regulated and driven by a causal architecture that integrated insights from the most empirically validated theories of the Neolithic transition, including theories from cognitive science, psychology, anthropology, sociology, economics, archaeology, and history (Shults and Wildman 2018). This methodology provides one way of contributing to Taves' and Asprem's goal of helping "scholars in the humanities and social sciences to bring psychological and neuroscientific research to bear on the phenomena they are studying" (p. 6).

We also developed an SDM that enabled us to simulate the transitional era in human civilization known as the "axial age", the period between approximately 800–200 BCE during which large-scale, literate societies characterized (*inter alia*) by competing coalitions of priestly elites and increasingly differentiated governmental institutions emerged in west, south, and east Asia (Shults, Wildman, *et al.* 2018). This model explicitly simulated the shift from pre-axial to axial *worldviews*, a shift that was driven by a computational architecture integrating the main pathways to axiality postulated in the relevant literatures in evolutionary psychology, energy capture, and historical sociology. Simulation experiments on the parameter space of this SDM shed light on the relative plausibility of competing theories about the axial age and on the conditions under which this sort of radical shift in worldview could occur in a population.

Of course, creating consilience through constructing computational models takes a great deal of effort. It requires scholars to be willing to engage disciplinary others and to outline their favoured theories with enough precision that they can be tested and contested. This process can test the patience and goodwill of even the most open-minded subject matter experts (and computer engineers). In our experience, however, CMS methodologies have provided a powerfully effective set of tools for facilitating collaborative multidisciplinary research on complex phenomena such as the formation and transmission worldviews. Insofar as these methodologies make reverse engineering easier for humanists and social scientists, they can contribute to Taves' and Asprem's goal of transforming the study of the mechanisms at work in worldviews commonly referred to as "religious" or "non-religious" through the BBA (Asprem 2014; Taves, Asprem, and Ihm 2018; Taves 2018a).

Finally, CMS can also contribute to the studious transformation of our own worldviews. By this I mean that the ongoing human attempt to answer the Big Questions (BQs) can itself be supported not only by the formal enhancement of human simulation capacities but also by the material insights provided by the actual process of conceptual and computational modelling. This holds for all of the BQs, but I will limit myself here to some brief comments on the first and the sixth, which are related to ontology and praxeology respectively.

What exists, what is real? Cognitive biases such as intuitive dualism and magical thinking undergird beliefs in immaterial souls that can escape from material bodies and in hidden supernatural agents that somehow transcend the causal nexus of the natural world. Philosophical defenders of these kinds of beliefs have sometimes argued that the incapacity of immanent, material causes to generate "higher" level phenomena such as intentionality or an ordered cosmos lends credibility to the existence of such spiritual entities. However, the fact that mathematical and computational modelling techniques can actually "grow" emergent wholes, with capacities that are irreducible to their parts, from the interaction of "lower" level components, weakens this apologetic move, and opens up the possibility of articulating a flat ontology within the context of a transcendence-free, naturalistic metaphysics in which morphogenesis is explained purely with mechanisms of immanence (DeLanda 2011; Rudrauf *et al.* 2017; Shults 2019a, 2019b).

What actions should we take? What path should we follow? At the individual level, each of us faces (and implicitly answers) these questions throughout life, whether or not we explicitly reflect on the praxeological dimension of our worldviews. At the institutional level, policy makers are charged with the task of constantly making these questions explicit and explicating their answers to them. One of most rapidly growing applications of CMS is in social simulation, which has been increasingly utilized by policy professionals in a wide variety of fields (Desai 2012; Jager and Edmonds 2015; Ahrweiler 2017). Despite their limitations, the relative effectiveness of these tools in addressing policy questions has led some leading scholars in this field to suggest that, at least in complex contexts where the risks in policy change are high, it would be unethical *not* to use them (Gilbert *et al.* 2018, Shults and Wildman 2019). The stakes may not always be so high in scientific research, but insofar as scholars accept the responsibility of pursuing knowledge as objectively and efficiently as possible, we can at least say that exploring CMS would be commendable, especially for those committed to achieving consilience across academic disciplines.

About the Author

F. LeRon Shults is Professor at the Institute for Global Development and Planning and director of the NORCE Center for Modelling Social Systems in Kristiansand, Norway. He has published 18 books and over 100 articles and book chapters on topics in philosophy, psychology, computer modelling, and the scientific study of religion. Shults' most recent book is *Practicing Safe Sects: Religious Reproduction in Scientific and Philosophical Perspective* (Brill, 2018).

References

Ahrweiler, Petra. 2017. "Agent-Based Simulation for Science, Technology, and Innovation Policy." *Scientometrics* 110(1): 391–415.
Asprem, Egil. 2014. *The Problem of Disenchantment: Scientific Naturalism and Esoteric Discourse, 1900-1939*. Leiden: Brill.
—2016. "Reverse-Engineering 'Esotericism': How to Prepare a Complex Cultural Concept for the Cognitive Science of Religion." *Religion* 46(2): 158–85.
Asprem, Egil, and Ann Taves. 2017. "Connecting Events: Experienced, Narrated, and Framed." *Religion, Brain & Behavior* 7(1): 88–93.
—2018a. "Explanation and the Study of Religion." Unpublished paper. Available from http://su.diva-portal.org/smash/get/diva2:1236674/FULLTEXT01.pdf
—2018b. "To our Critics." In *Method Today: Redescribing Approaches to the Study of Religion*, edited by Brad Stoddard, 192–201. Sheffield, UK: Equinox.
Bechtel, William. 2009. "Looking Down, Around, and Up: Mechanistic Explanation in Psychology." *Philosophical Psychology* 22(5): 543–64.
Benioff, Marc R., and Edward D. Lazowska. 2005. "Computational Science: Ensuring America's Competitiveness." National Coordination Office for Information Technology Research & Development. Available from https://www.nitrd.gov/pitac/reports/20050609_computational/computational.pdf
Conte, Rosaria, Giulia Andrighetto, and Marco Campennì. 2014. *Minding Norms: Mechanisms and Dynamics of Social Order in Agent Societies*. Oxford: Oxford University Press.
Dávid-Barrett, Tamás, and James Carney. 2015. "The Deification of Historical Figures and the Emergence of Priesthoods as a Solution to a Network Coordination Problem." *Religion, Brain & Behavior* 6(4): 307–17.
DeLanda, Manuel. 2011. *Philosophy and Simulation: The Emergence of Synthetic Reason*. London: Continuum.
Desai, Anand, ed. 2012. *Simulation for Public Policy*. New York: Springer.
Dignum, Frank, and Virginia Dignum. 2014. *Perspectives on Culture and Agent-Based Simulations: Integrating Cultures*. Cham: Springer.
Friston, Karl. 2018. "Am I Self-Conscious? (Or Does Self-Organization Entail Self-Consciousness?)." *Frontiers in Psychology* 9: 579. https://doi.org/10.3389/fpsyg.2018.00579
Gilbert, Nigel, Petra Ahrweiler, Pete Barbrook-Johnson, Kavin P. Narasimhan, and Helen Wilkinson. 2018. "Computational Modelling of Public Policy." *Journal of Artificial Societies and Social Simulation* 21(1): 1–19.
Gore, Ross, Carlos Lemos, F. LeRon Shults, and Wesley J. Wildman. 2018. "Forecasting Changes in Religiosity and Existential Security with an Agent-Based Model." *Journal of Artificial Societies and Social Simulation* 21: 1–31.
Gratch, Jonathan, and Stacy Marsella. 2014. *Social Emotions in Nature and Artifact*. Oxford: Oxford University Press.
Hamill, Lynne, and Nigel Gilbert. 2015. *Agent-Based Modelling in Economics*. New York: John Wiley & Sons.

Hassan, Samer, Javier Arroyo, José Manuel Galan, Luis Antunes, and Juan Pavón. 2013. "Asking the Oracle: Introducing Forecasting Principles into Agent-Based Modelling." *The Journal of Artificial Societies and Social Simulation* 16(3) online. https://doi.org/10.18564/jasss.2241

Hauke, Jonas, Iris Lorscheid, and Matthias Meyer. 2017. "Recent Development of Social Simulation as Reflected in JASSS between 2008 and 2014: A Citation and Co-Citation Analysis." *The Journal of Artificial Societies and Social Simulation* 20(1) online. https://doi.org/10.18564/jasss.3238

Jager, Wander, and Bruce Edmonds. 2015. "Policy Making and Modelling in a Complex World." In *Policy Practice and Digital Science*, edited by Marijn Janssen, Maria A. Wimmer, and Ameneh Deljoo, 57–73. Cham: Springer.

Lane, Justin E. 2019. "Bridging Qualitative and Quantitative Approaches to Religion." *Religion, Brain & Behavior* 9(3): 301–307. https://doi.org/10.1080/2153599X.2018.1429008

Mascaro, Steven. 2010. *Evolving Ethics: The New Science of Good and Evil*. Exeter: Imprint Academic. Available from http://hdl.handle.net/2027/inu.30000127033425

Matthews, Luke J., Jeffrey Edmonds, Wesley J. Wildman, and Charles L. Nunn. 2013. "Cultural Inheritance or Cultural Diffusion of Religious Violence? A Quantitative Case Study of the Radical Reformation." *Religion, Brain & Behavior* 3(1): 3–15.

Miller, John H. 2007. *Complex Adaptive Systems: An Introduction to Computational Models of Social Life*. Princeton, NJ: Princeton University Press.

Nielbo, Kristoffer L., Donald M. Braxton, and Afzal Upal. 2012. "Computing Religion: A New Tool in the Multilevel Analysis of Religion." *Method and Theory in the Study of Religion* 24(3): 267–90.

Roitto, Rikard. 2015. "Dangerous but Contagious Altruism: Recruitment of Group Members and Reform of Cooperation Style through Altruism in Two Modified Versions of Hammond and Axelrod's Simulation of Ethnocentric Cooperation." *Religion, Brain & Behavior* 5(3): 154–68.

Rudrauf, David, Daniel Bennequin, Isabela Granic, Gregory Landini, Karl Friston, and Kenneth Williford. 2017. "A Mathematical Model of Embodied Consciousness." *Journal of Theoretical Biology* 428(C): 106–31. https://doi.org/10.1016/j.jtbi.2017.05.032

Shults, F. LeRon. 2015. "How to Survive the Anthropocene: Adaptive Atheism and the Evolution of Homo Deiparensis." *Religions* 6(2): 724–41.

—2018. *Practicing Safe Sects: Religious Reproduction in Scientific and Philosophical Perspective*. Leiden: Brill Academic.

—2019a. "Modeling Metaphysics: The Rise of Simulation and the Reversal of Platonism." *Proceedings of the 2019 Spring Simulation Conference*: 1–12.

—2019b. "Computer Modeling in Philosophy of Religion." *Open Philosophy* 2(1): 108–25. https://doi.org/10.1515/opphil-2019-0011

—2019c. "Simulating Supernatural Seeking." *Religion, Brain & Behavior* 9(3): 262–65. https://doi.org/10.1080/2153599X.2018.1453530

Shults, F. LeRon, Ross Gore, Carlos Lemos, and Wesley J. Wildman. 2018. "Why Do the Godless Prosper? Modeling the Cognitive and Coalitional Mechanisms that Promote Atheism." *Psychology of Religion and Spirituality* 10(3): 218–28.

Shults, F. LeRon, Ross Gore, Wesley J. Wildman, Christopher Lynch, Justin E. Lane, and Monica Toft. 2018. "A Generative Model of the Mutual Escalation of Anxiety between Religious Groups." *Journal of Artificial Societies and Social Simulation* 21(4) online. https://doi.org/10.18564/jasss.3840

Shults, F. LeRon, Justin E. Lane, Saikou Diallo, Christopher Lynch, Wesley J. Wildman, and Ross Gore. 2018. "Modeling Terror Management Theory: Computer Simulations of the Impact of Mortality Salience on Religiosity." *Religion, Brain & Behavior* 8(1): 77–100.

Shults, F. LeRon, and Wesley J. Wildman. 2018. "Simulating Religious Entanglement and Social Investment in the Neolithic." In *Religion, History and Place in the Origin of Settled Life*, edited by Ian Hodder, 33–63. Colorado Springs, CO: University of Colorado Press.

—2019. "Ethics, Computer Simulation, and the Future of Humanity." In *Human Simulation: Perspectives, Insights and Applications*, edited by Saikou Diallo, Wesley J. Wildman, F. LeRon Shults, and Andreas Tolk, 21–40. Berlin: Springer.

Shults, F. LeRon, Wesley J. Wildman, Justin E. Lane, Christopher Lynch, and Saikou Diallo. 2018. "Multiple Axialities: A Computational Model of the Axial Age." *Journal of Cognition and Culture* 18: 537–64.

Sun, Ron. 2001. *Duality of the Mind: A Bottom-up Approach toward Cognition*. Hove, UK: Psychology Press.

Sun, Ron, and Robert Mathews. 2012. "Implicit Cognition, Emotion, and Meta-Cognitive Control." *Mind & Society* 11(1): 107–19.

Taves, Ann. 2015. "Reverse Engineering Complex Cultural Concepts: Identifying Building Blocks of 'Religion'." *Journal of Cognition and Culture* 15(1-2): 191–216.

—2018a. "Finding and Articulating Meaning in Secular Experience." In *Religious Experience and Experiencing Religion in Religious Education*, edited by Ulrich Riegel, Eva-Maria Leven, and Daniel Fleming, 13–22. Münster: Waxman.

—2019a. "Modeling Theories and Modeling Phenomena: A Humanist's Initiation." In *Human Simulation: Perspectives, Insights and Applications*, edited by Saikou Diallo, Wesley J. Wildman, F. LeRon Shults, and Andreas Tolk, 83–94. Cham: Springer.

—2019b. "(Revelatory) Events: A Response to Commentators." *Religion, Brain & Behavior* 9(3): 307–11. https://doi.org/10.1080/2153599X.2018.1429013

Taves, Ann, and Egil Asprem. 2017. "Experience as Event: Event Cognition and the Study of (Religious) Experiences." *Religion, Brain & Behavior* 7(1): 43–62.

Taves, Ann, Egil Asprem, and Elliott Ihm. 2018. "Psychology, Meaning Making, and the Study of Worldviews: Beyond Religion and Non-Religion." *Psychology of Religion and Spirituality* 10(3): 207–17.

Tolk, Andreas. 2012. *Engineering Principles of Combat Modeling and Distributed Simulation*. New York: John Wiley.

—2015. "Learning Something Right from Models that are Wrong: Epistemology of Simulation." In *Concepts and Methodologies for Modeling and Simulation*, edited by Levant Yilmaz, 87–106. Cham: Springer.

Upal, M.A. 2005. "Simulating the Emergence of New Religious Movements." *Journal of Artificial Societies and Social Simulation* 8(1) online.

Whitehouse, Harvey, Ken Kahn, Michael E. Hochberg, and Joanna J. Bryson. 2012. "The Role for Simulations in Theory Construction for the Social Sciences: Case Studies Concerning Divergent Modes of Religiosity." *Religion, Brain & Behaviour* 2(3): 182–201.

Wildman, Wesley J., Paul A. Fishwick, and F. LeRon Shults. 2017. "Teaching at the Intersection of Simulation and the Humanities." In *Proceedings of the 2017 Winter Simulation Conference*, edited by Wai Kin Victor Chan, 1–13.

Youngman, Paul A., and Mirsad Hadzikadic. 2014. *Complexity and the Human Experience: Modeling Complexity in the Humanities and Social Sciences*. Abingdon: Pan Stanford.

8

Comments and Reflections

Ann Taves
University of California, CA

Egil Asprem
Stockholm University

The six chapters fall neatly into two groups. The first group (Larsson, Nordin, and Feldt) raises a series of challenges and the second group (Svensson, Visuri, and Shults) charts new directions. We will respond to the challenges raised by the former group and highlight key innovations in the latter group.

Challenges

Göran Larsson's wonderful opening chapter on the reception and debate over the BBA aptly describes the cross currents we have attempted to navigate. As he so clearly points out, many of the sharpest criticisms of our efforts negate one another: we are criticized as insufficiently "constructionist" or insufficiently "scientific", for "essentializing religion" and for refusing to define it, and for maintaining a place for meaning and values in the academy and refusing to consider meaning and values. Rather than rehearse our views on these issues, which he accurately represents, we will comment on Larsson's very helpful suggestions for moving forward. In doing so, Larsson relies on D'Andrade's (1995: 399) distinction between subjective and objective description and Boyer's (2011: 7–10) distinction between naturalistic and erudite modes. Both have important implications for relating and/or bridging between the humanities and the sciences.

Larsson introduces D'Andrade's distinction between an "objective description [which] tells about the thing described, not about the agent doing the description" and a "subjective description [which] tells how the agent doing the description reacts to the object" (1995: 399) in the context of a discussion of the place of matters of "meaning and value" in the context of the university. Larsson quotes Martin and Wiebe's rejoinder (2012b) to Taves' response (2012) to an initial article by Martin and Wiebe (2012a). In their rejoinder, Martin and Wiebe interpret Taves as arguing that "the objective of achieving an exclusively scientific (i.e., causal) explanation for religious thought and behaviour is inappropriate to the subject matter of 'religious studies'". She was actually trying to make a more forceful point, to wit: "the objective of achieving an *exclusively* scientific (i.e., causal) explanation for [human] thought and behaviour is inappropriate to the subject matter of [the university]". Her point was not to downplay the importance of explanatory approaches to the study of religion, but to insist that the university cannot forego the task of reflecting on questions of meaning and value nor escape the fact that higher education plays a role in the "formation" of students as citizens or critical thinkers or moral agents, whether we reflect on that process or not. Reflecting on systems of meaning and value need not mean advocating particular systems; reflecting can mean critical reflection on meaning and value, particularly in relation to the effects and outcomes of various human behaviours. So, for example, in addition to analysing and explaining how certain forms of self-cultivation might work, we can also investigate their effects on human well-being and the ability to function in the world, individually and collectively, in light of various normative and ethical frameworks. The importance of such reflection promises to become ever more apparent as the efforts of the US Department of Defense (DARPA) in creating technologically enhanced humans become more available to the general public (on this see, e.g., Garreau 2005).

We can think of empirical research into various phenomena as asking interpretive, explanatory, or prospective questions and producing rich analytic descriptions (interpretation), scientific explanations, and/or studies of effects and outcomes (predictions). The first two correspond to what Boyer (2011: 7–10) meant by the scientific and erudite modes. "While the first mode", as Larsson explains, "strives for naturalistic explanations that are based on empirical observations, the other mode is focused more on describing and systematizing the empirical data" (p. 34). Critical, ethical reflection can focus both on the effects and outcomes of past behaviour (e.g. in relation to the environment, diplomacy, technological advances) or on anticipated effects and outcomes of future behaviour (e.g. in relation to global warming, technological enhancement). We might even want to make and defend the normative claim that policy decisions *should* be made on the basis of evidence.

D'Andrade's point in distinguishing between objective and subjective definitions was not that critical reflection on values did not belong in the academy, but that "any moral authority that anthropologists may hold depends upon an objective understanding of the world and to that end moral and objective models should be kept distinct" (1995: 399). We agree with D'Andrade on this point and with Martin and Wiebe (2012b) when they say, "that if the study of religion is to be scientific, it must clearly distinguish the epistemological from the axiological and theological concerns that now dominate the discipline". The key here, we would submit, is not to eliminate critical reflection on meaning and values from the university but to engage in the formation of students who are able to (1) distinguish between epistemological and axiological claims, (2) weigh the publicly available evidence for epistemological claims, and (3) reflect critically on those behaviours in relation to various axiological frameworks. We hope that a focus on the "big questions" that animate worldviews and ways of life will help students learn to make these distinctions and assess them more critically.

In his chapter on counterintuitive supernaturalism as a building block of religious dream imagery, Andreas Nordin rightly points out that the BBA is one among a number of cognitive approaches that assume that "religion ... encompass[es] a broad range of different phenomena that should be 'fractionated' into constitutive parts better suited for scientific investigation" (p. 55). He is also right to observe that such an approach is widely assumed in CSR circles and, thus, in that context the BBA may be "forcing an open door". Indeed, we have received little pushback in the CSR community for adopting this approach.

Although the BBA shares this assumption with numerous other CSR approaches, we think that the BBA nonetheless has some distinctive emphases that reflect our training and work as historians and our shared interest in unusual experiences. The former led us to put greater stress on the process whereby constitutive parts are reassembled (i.e. historical development) than some approaches and the latter to a focus on events (aka experiences) as a core concept alongside representations (aka beliefs) and actions (aka practices, rituals). Moreover, due to our respective training in the "history of religions" and the "history of Western esotericism", we are also acutely aware of the role of complex cultural concepts in defining fields of inquiry and the difficulties these can present for empirical research. Thus, perhaps more than other approaches, we have stressed the idea that the components of things deemed religious can be assembled into phenomena that may be deemed otherwise, for example, as esoteric, spiritual, fictional, or superstitious. Hence our concern with appraisal processes at multiple levels – including the level of academic disciplines – which we drew initially from social psychology and subsequently expanded.

We can illustrate the effects of these differences in relation to Nordin's impressive ethnographic research on dreams in Nepal. As he points out, his focus on "counterintuitive supernaturalism" builds on MCI theory, which holds that "violations of intuitive expectation, such as breaches and transfers of basic ontological categories (e.g. Boyer 1994, 2001; Barrett 2000, 2004; Pyysiäinen 2001)" (p. 62). MCI theory dates to the beginnings of CSR and, thus, long predates the BBA. Yet, while MCI theory predicts that people are more likely to remember counterintuitive aspects of dreams, it does not explain, as Nordin acknowledges, "why *supernatural* and counterintuitive agency would be a preferred imaginary construct in religious dreaming" (p. 61). Our stress on "religion" as a CCC would lead us to mind the gap, so to speak, between counterintuitive agents, defined in terms of a blending of cognitively intuitive categories, and agents with properties that people – including researchers – characterize as supernatural, paranormal, superstitious, or magical. Not minding this gap, as Lindeman and Svedholm (2012) demonstrate, has led to independent lines of psychological research on each of these cultural concepts as if they were not all counterintuitive in the psychological sense. So while we applaud Nordin's investigation of counterintuitive imagery in the dreams of Nepalese villagers, we would be interested in whether MCI features predicted which dreams would be considered special and whether special dreams were more prevalent at religious than nonreligious sites. We would also be interested in local systems of dream classification and interpretation and whether dreamers and local experts ever differed in their assessments. These questions all relate to how people decide what dreams are special both in terms of salience and significance. It is possible that dreams with MCI concepts are salient but not particularly significant unless the MCI concepts fall into culturally significant categories. This raises the further question of how people know what is happening in their dreams (and elsewhere).

Our emphasis on experiences, including dreams, as events provides a theoretical basis for exploring the question of how people know what is happening both while it is happening and after the fact (Taves and Asprem 2017). As noted in our overview of the BBA, event cognition refers to a set of mechanisms that allow us to form mental representations of what is going on around us and segment the flow of information into discrete, bounded events (Radvansky and Zacks 2014). A dream is such an event. Because we make use of event models not only when determining what is going on around us, but also when remembering past events, planning future events, telling a fictional story, or understanding a story told to us by others, this research would lead us to expect some level of congruence between experiences as they occur and our immediate accounts of them. Dreams, more than any other type of experience, highlight the fact that seemingly real events can occur internally (in the absence of external sensory stimulation) and that event models give us access to how an event was perceived by a subject and not the (internal or external) stimuli alone. Specifically, the theory indicates that event models are the brain's predictions based on the interaction between stimuli and the schemas they elicit.

Drawing on this theoretical model and recognizing that there is always a gap between an event and its narration, we have developed methods (see Asprem and Taves forthcoming) for analysing narratives, which if applied to dream narratives, would allow Nordin to gain insight into the way sensations are appraised in the dream and dream content appraised after the fact. Thus, for example in the first dream, it is possible that bodily sensations generated a sense of "uplift" to which a "bus-flying" schema was attached. "Upward" movement was associated with heaven, deities, and a different world where everyone was sitting chanting mantras. The content of the dream suggests that culturally salient schemas regarding heaven, deities, and devotional practice were all attached to a sense of upward movement. The counterintuitive element of a flying bus may have made the dream salient, but the associated schemas made it significant. In the second dream, we could imagine an example in which the person was burnt and died, as in this dream, but instead of a supernatural serpent initiating the action, unknown persons initiated it, or perhaps it just happened without any causal agent. In all cases, the person might be surprised, even while they were still in the dream, to discover that the fire did not burn their body, but the significance of the dream would likely depend on the dreamer's ability to find meaning in it. By asking dreamers how significant they felt the dream was upon waking, whether they shared it with others, and how they assessed it later, we think Nordin could learn more about the role MCI concepts play in the dreams people view as most significant.

Laura Feldt raises a number of very important issues that we are happy to address, because – like her – we are trying to work on both sides of the humanities–sciences divide. First, we think her "foreground-background" distinction with regard to narratives is very helpful and we agree that the BBA focuses primarily on the "background". We started there for reasons we can elaborate, but did so as historians with the "foreground" in mind. Second, we agree that the BBA needs further elaboration along the lines suggested by Feldt and have some ideas for doing so. Finally, we will take up the "worldviews" versus "religions" question, where again we share the larger goal of broadening our field of investigation, but differ on how we might best go about that.

Background-Foreground: To take up Feldt's first point, the BBA does focus on the "background", that is, what happens behind narratives, because (1) we were trying to construct a bridge between the sciences and the humanities and (2) we were hoping to reintroduce "experience" as a subject for study in the wake of the critiques of the late twentieth century. When we recast "experiences" as "events" in our more recent formulations of the BBA, we did so with an eye to both the "background" and the "foreground" and thus many of the issues Feldt raises. Relative to the background, we think that "event cognition" as a high-level form of unconscious processing (Butz and Kutter 2017) provides an effective bridge between subconscious mental processing and the narratives with which historians work for several reasons: first, narratives typically recount an event or series of events; second, research on event cognition suggests that event models in the mind of the narrator and the listeners are similar (not identical) at the point at which the narrative is recounted; and, third, event models draw together all the aspects of an event that are *relevant* to the narrator. Each of these points has implications for historians, which leads us to how this might be elaborated.

Elaborations: (1) Because narratives typically recount an event or series of events, we can use various methods to dissect and compare multiple versions over time. We have developed methods for doing this, which we have used to extract data from historical narratives (Taves 2016; Taves and Harper 2016) and will be included as a "technique" in the second edition of the *Handbook of Research Methods in the Study of Religion* (Asprem and Taves forthcoming). (2) Experimental researchers have pushed back, arguing that our historical reconstructions are not as reliable as their experimental evidence (Schjødt 2018). We recognize that event models in the mind of narrators and listeners are not identical, but because narratives are always recounted in a context (even if a laboratory context), historians are well equipped to bring the context to the fore when studying the recounting of narratives. (3) Because both event cognition research and historians view events as drawing together all the aspects of an event that are *relevant* to the narrator in a particular *situation*, we think that it can easily be elaborated to explicitly include the role of media and materiality and other aspects of the situation that are readily apparent to historians. Though we have not tackled this yet, we think that event cognition has the potential to offer psychological and evolutionary underpinnings (background) to "practice theory" (Rouse 2006) as articulated in the social sciences and widely embraced in the humanities (foreground), thus building a sturdier and more elaborated "bridge". We also note that Christian Smith (2017) has recently advanced a theory of religion built around an attributional approach to events. If we bracket the issue of defining religion, which we are resisting, his approach is highly compatible with what we have been advocating.

Religion versus Worldviews: This takes us to the third issue, whether we would be "better off using a broad concept of religion rather than a concept of worldviews to guide our analyses of the material" (p. 47). Feldt suggests two contexts in which she thinks "religion" is more helpful: ancient Mesopotamia and contemporary media and popular culture. Ironically, these are two contexts in which we think adopting "worldviews and ways of life" as our second-order conceptual framework is more helpful than a broad second-order concept of "religion".

Before explaining the advantages from a "foreground" perspective, let us highlight the "background" reasons we are advocating placing "religion" or "religions" under the wider rubric of worldviews and ways of life. In doing so, we are assuming, like Feldt and many others in our field, that religion is a subset of culture. In keeping with our bridging intentions, however, we want to ground the aspect of culture that seems to be of most interest to scholars of religion in an evolutionary perspective. This does two things: (1) it creates a strong bridge to the sciences, allowing us to trace the evolutionary capacity to generate worldviews in conjunction with the increased capacity to cognize events and (2), in so far as answering the "big questions" (BQs) is a panhuman capacity, the questions provide a stable platform for making comparisons across cultures, traditions, and ways of life.

With respect to the ancient Mesopotamia and other contexts without an explicit concept of "religion", we think that the BQs offer a stable platform for setting up comparisons in contexts that do have an explicit concept of religion. Thus, to use her example, "obtaining this-worldly goals – a good harvest, a successful battle, healing for a sick child" (p. 48) are perfectly good answers to the axiology BQ (What is the good [the goal] for which we should strive?). Although Feldt argues that we must fall back on "long-standing scholarly discussions of religion ... to guide us when we study fields that have no explicit discourses on religion, magic, or the sacred" (p. 48), we are suggesting that the BQs offer such a guide. The praxeology question (What do we need to do to reach the goal?) offers the opportunity to explore the practices, objects, techniques that are required in order to achieve a good harvest, a successful battle, or a healed child. These can be located against the backdrop of the other BQs: the ontology question (What exists? What is real?), the cosmology question (Who am I? Who are we? Where do we come from? Where are we going?), the epistemology question (How do we know this – about ourselves and reality more generally?), and the situation question (What is the situation in which we find ourselves? What is our nature?). As we explore how ancient Mesopotamians or others answer these questions, we can also ask how *they* (actors in the field) conceptualized the practices in question and how their goals and practices were reconceptualized (e.g. as magic, religion, etc.) in contact situations, whether in their own time or later.

The contemporary situation provides another interesting test case. Here Feldt rightly highlights the way that "religion" (as conceived and disestablished in the West) is "thinly spread out, and thoroughly mixed with other things like entertainment, commerce, and play" (p. 41) in popular culture. Although, as she indicates, "actors in the field" encompass much of this under the heading of "spirituality", Feldt here too argues that we need to use an explicit concept of religion to avoid defaulting to an implicit one. Here again, we would counter that the BQs not only provide such a tool, but allow us to explore the wide range of phenomena of interest to Feldt and others under a comparative rubric that does not redescribe the non- or anti-religious as religious (Taves, Asprem, and Ihm 2018). Where we feel our approach does need more elaboration is in relation to what we are calling modes of worldview expression (enacted, expressed, memorized, and textualized), scale (individual, family, community, society), and scope of expression (very context specific to highly generalized). Scope opens the question of the extent to which answers to the BQs are very situation specific (i.e. related to a specific action or event) or generalized to a greater or lesser extent across situations (Taves unpublished). Investigating the interaction between modes, scale, and scope is particularly important in complex societies where sources are readily available. Doing so should allow us to better conceptualize the changes that take place in situations of contact, whether migration, conflict, colonization, or conquest. These are matters that we want to develop more in the future.

New Directions

Jonas Svensson's study of the Qur'an highlights the multi-level character of the BBA and the way that multi-level theories can be tested using textual data. In introducing his chapter, Svensson notes two important features of the BBA: it presupposes multiple levels of building blocks and conceives of building blocks as composites. Although these presuppositions were implicit in the initial formulation of the BBA (Taves 2009, since republished in 2011), we are now explicitly grounding them philosophically in the "new mechanistic" approach to explanation in the philosophy of science. In this approach, building blocks are *components that interact* to produce a phenomenon. The interacting components are the *mechanism* that produces the phenomenon. Each of the building blocks is itself a composite or, as the new mechanists would say, a phenomenon in its own right, produced through the interaction of its own components (or building blocks). The new mechanists, thus, refer to *levels of mechanisms*, which we could equally well describe as levels of phenomena or levels of building blocks, nested in stacks.

This means, as Svensson rightly points out, that researchers can select a phenomenon to analyse and explain at whatever level they find interesting.

Svensson's chapter illustrates how a building block (or new mechanistic) approach can be adopted as a way of thinking about how things work, and then used to recognize theories that explain phenomena through the interaction of components and test them in light of relevant evidence with which the researcher is familiar. Svensson identified Moral Foundations Theory (as developed by Haidt 2012; Graham et al. 2013), as taking such an approach, since it holds that five evolved moral intuitions interact to produce variations in norms across cultures. Because methods have been developed to test it using textual sources, he was able to use these methods to determine if these methods would distinguish translations of the Qur'an that are viewed as more conservative and more liberal. As Svensson rightly notes, researchers are developing many such theories, most of which originate outside the field of religious studies and, thus, have not typically been developed with religions in mind. In a spirit of consilience, he urges scholars in the humanities to engage with such theories and test them in light of the materials they know best. This is an aim we too would heartily endorse.

Ingela Visuri's study of "embodied supernatural experience" in young adults on the high-functioning autism spectrum is an exemplary illustration of what a BBA can look like in practice. It also highlights how the BBA differs from a more traditional CSR approach. Taking a bottom-up approach to complex cultural concepts such as "religion" and "autism" allowed Visuri to break with the essentializing and stereotyped views of autism that remain influential in CSR studies of religion and autism, and shift her focus from "supernatural beliefs" to "experiences" that individuals deemed significant and attributed to various non-ordinary agents. Moreover, Visuri's mix of quantitative psychological research methods with a qualitative study of the subjects' emic attributions and sense-making led to the intriguing discovery that millennials on the autism spectrum were drawing on characters and concepts from popular occulture when they sought to make sense of baffling somatosensory experiences. Interviews also revealed that informants tended to be fully aware that the agents they interacted with, whether characters from the Transformers movies or the Harry Potter universe, were entirely fictional. A traditional CSR approach that applies concepts of "religion" and "supernatural beliefs" might easily have distorted these narratives, missed the important nuances in individuals' attributions, and – in our view – likely failed to discover the multi-level causal mechanisms that produce these phenomena.

This leads us to reflect on the multi-level model that Visuri proposes for unusual sensory experiences in autism. While she explicitly bases it on Armin Geertz's (2010) biocultural model, which represented a metatheoretical framework of "religion" on four "levels of reality", we find that Visuri's model departs from Geertz's in important ways that make it more congruent with our recent reformulation of the BBA in terms of nested mechanisms. There are two key differences, namely, in *what* we model, and in how we conceptualize *levels*. Geertz offers a model of "religion", based on his stipulated definition of religion as "a cultural system and a social institution that governs and promotes ideal interpretations of existence and ideal praxis with reference to postulated transempirical powers or beings" (Geertz 2010: 305). The BBA is characteristically open-ended and interested in modelling multi-level appraisal processes whether or not the appraisals are deemed "religious" or involve "transempirical beings". Visuri's model is, we think, a great example of the latter: it illustrates how appraisal processes in the shape of signalling errors on the neurotransmitter level are expressed as atypical sensory processing and give rise to anomalous experiences on the conscious level. These then spark a psychological sense-making process that draws on available cultural resources.

Visuri's model tacitly breaks with the conception of levels embedded in Geertz's model. Instead of identifying "levels of reality" (which we suspect is really based on a common hierarchical ordering of various *disciplines* from the "fundamental" hard sciences to the "complex" soft humanities), her model suggests levels of *mechanisms*, in keeping with the way we are conceptualizing the BBA in terms of new mechanism. As discussed earlier, this is to say (1) that we seek the parts that interact to produce some phenomenon of interest, irrespective of whether those parts are studied by sociologists, neuroscientist, or chemists, and (2) that we do this in full knowledge that each interacting part can itself be described as a mechanism consisting of other interacting parts.

We think that this view of levels is a better fit with Visuri's actual research practice. It is not, for example, the case that occultural attributions (cultural/discursive level) simply supervene (in the ontological sense) on signalling errors (neurological level), as a "levels of reality" reading of the model might suggest. Instead, Visuri's particular phenomenon of interest is the attribution process of individuals on the autism spectrum, and she proposes a multi-level *mechanism* that tries to explain that phenomenon. On a levels of mechanism view, occultural schemas are in this case not placed on a "higher" cultural level from the psychological, but rather *components in* psychological sense-making that *interact* with atypical sensory processing to produce the anomalous event as experienced and appraised. Once again, it is crucial to remember that levels of mechanisms are relative to a phenomenon of interest. We can, for instance, also look at the occultural schemas as represented in the minds of the informants as our phenomenon of interest, and focus on how they were learned through a mechanism of occultural socialization that involves, for example, gaming practice and group interaction in online fandom forums. This is just one example of how Visuri's research provides a stimulating way to think about the BBA and new mechanism in a practical research context that brings to light complex causal relationships in everyday praxis.

As LeRon Shults' references to our collaborative ventures suggest, we are enthusiastically on board with the idea of modelling and testing a BBA to worldviews and we deeply appreciate his humanities-friendly description of what that might entail. In his overview of the "new mechanistic philosophy", we particularly appreciate his use of Bechtel (2009) to stress that "to make sense of the relevant mechanisms", we need to "look around" at the way they are organized and "look up" at the situation in which they are embedded, as well as "look down" to identify the component parts. This is something we have recognized intuitively but have not stated explicitly. Shults' awareness, we suspect, comes not simply from reading Bechtel, but from the actual work of modelling mechanisms, where "looking down" alone was insufficient.

Moreover, although we have expressed our interest in modelling the processes at the heart of worldview construction and maintenance, this is Shults' first attempt to characterize what that might entail. We are heartened to learn that there is so much that we could build on in constructing such a model. To some extent, this might entail reframing what other models are doing. For example, the model that Shults *et al.* (2018) conceived as modelling the mutual escalation of anxiety (and thus conflict) between groups might also be used to model the role of anxiety in the polarization of worldviews. Similarly, the model that Gore *et al.* (2018) developed to demonstrate macro-level shifts in non-religiosity under certain conditions could be used to model the shift from religious to secular worldviews. We are excited at the thought that agent-based models might allow us to "grow" societies with divergent worldviews. Finally, the two system-dynamic models, which Shults explicitly describes as modelling shifts in ways of life (the Neolithic transition) and worldviews (the axial-age transition) provide a base for determining under what conditions ways of life develop into explicit worldviews, are systematized by specialists, and transformed through interactions with others. Although it is easy enough to frame these models in terms of worldview dynamics, the challenge will be to (1) operationalize the interactions between the BQs and (2) define rules for their elaboration.

About the Authors

Ann Taves is Distinguished Professor of religious studies at the University of California at Santa Barbara, Santa Barbara, CA.

Egil Asprem is Associate Professor of the history of religions at Stockholm University. His diverse research interests circle around the history of Western esotericism and new religious movements, with an emphasis on the implications of theoretical and methodological work in the social and cognitive sciences for these fields. His recent publications include *The Problem of Disenchantment: Scientific Naturalism and Esoteric Discourse* (Brill, 2014/SUNY, 2018) and the *Brill Handbook of Conspiracy Theory and Contemporary Religion* (Brill, 2018; co-edited with Asbjørn Dyrendal and David G. Robertson).

References

Asprem, Egil, and Ann Taves. Forthcoming. "Event Model Analysis." In *Routledge Handbook of Research Methods in the Study of Religion* (2nd edn), edited by Steven Engler and Michael Stausberg. London: Routledge.

Barrett, Justin L. 2000. "Exploring the Natural Foundations of Religion." *Trends in Cognitive Sciences* 4(1): 29–34.

—2004. *Why Would Anyone Believe in God?* Walnut Creek: Altamira Press.

Bechtel, William. 2009. *Mental Mechanisms: Philosophical Perspectives on Cognitive Neuroscience*. New York: Psychology Press.

Boyer, Pascal. 1994. *The Naturalness of Religious Ideas: A Cognitive Theory of Religion*. Berkeley, CA: University of California Press.

—2001. *Religion Explained: The Evolutionary Origins of Religious Thought*. New York: Basic Books.

—2011. "From Studious Irrelevancy to Consilient Knowledge: Modes of Scholarship and Cultural Anthropology." In *Creating Consilience: Evolution, Cognitive Science, and the Humanities*, edited by Edward Slingerland and Mark Collard, 113–29. Oxford: Oxford University Press.

Butz, Martin V., and Ester F. Kutter. 2017. *How the Mind Comes into Being: Introducing Cognitive Science from a Functional and Computational Perspective*. New York: Oxford University Press.

D'Andrade, Roy. 1995. "Moral Models in Anthropology." *Current Anthropology* 36(3): 399–408.

Garreau, Joel. 2005. *Radical Evolution: The Promise and Peril of Enhancing our Minds, our Bodies – and What it Means to be Human*. New York: Broadway Book.

Geertz, Armin. W. 2010. "Brain, Body and Culture: A Biocultural Theory of Religion." *Method and Theory in the Study of Religion* 22: 304–21.

Gore, Ross, Carlos Lemos, F. LeRon Shults, and Wesley J. Wildman. 2018. "Forecasting Changes in Religiosity and Existential Security with an Agent-Based Model." *Journal of Artificial Societies and Social Simulation* 21: 1–31.

Graham, Jesse, Jonathan Haidt, Sena Koleva, Matt Motyl, Ravi Iyer, Sean P. Wojcik, and Peter H. Ditto. 2013. "Moral Foundations Theory: The Pragmatic Validity of Moral Pluralism." *Advances in Experimental Social Psychology* 47: 55–130.

Haidt, Jonathan. 2012. *The Righteous Mind: Why Good People are Divided by Politics and Religion*. London: Allen Lane.

Lindeman, Marjaana, and Annika M. Svedholm. 2012. "What's in a Term? Paranormal, Superstitious, Magical and Supernatural Beliefs by Any Other Name Would Mean the Same." *Review of General Psychology* 16(3): 241–55.

Martin, Luther H., and Donald Wiebe. 2012a. "Religious Studies as a Scientific Discipline: The Persistence of a Delusion." *Journal of the American Academy of Religion* 80(3): 587–97.

—2012b. "When Pessimism is Realism: A Rejoinder to our Colleagues." *Journal of the American Academy of Religion* 80(3): 618–22.

Pyysiäinen, Ilkka. 2001. *How Religion Works: Towards a New Cognitive Science of Religion*. Leiden: Brill.

Radvansky, Gabriel A., and Jeffrey M. Zacks. 2014. *Event Cognition*. New York: Oxford University Press.

Rouse, Joseph. 2006. "Practice Theory." In *Philosophy of Anthropology and Sociology*, edited by Stephen Turner and Mark Risjord, 499–540. London: North Holland.

Schjødt, Uffe. 2018. "Predictive Coding in the Study of Religion: A Believer's Testimony." In *A New Synthesis: Cognition, Evolution, and History in the Study of Religion*, edited by Anders Klostergaard Petersen, Gilhus Ingvild Sælid, Luther H. Martin, Jeppe Sinding Jensen, and Jesper Sørensen, 364–79. Leiden: Brill.

Shults, F. LeRon, Ross Gore, Carlos Lemos, and Wesley J. Wildman. 2018. "Why Do the Godless Prosper? Modeling the Cognitive and Coalitional Mechanisms That Promote Atheism." *Psychology of Religion and Spirituality* 10(3): 218–28.

Smith, Christian. 2017. *Religion: What it is, How it Works, and Why it Matters*. Princeton, NJ: Princeton University Press.

Taves, Ann. 2011 [2009]. *Religious Experience Reconsidered: A Building-Block Approach to the Study of Religion and Other Special Things*. Princeton, NJ: Princeton University Press.

—2012. "A Response to Martin and Wiebe." *Journal of the American Academy of Religion* 80(3): 601–604.

—2016. *Revelatory Events: Three Case Studies of the Emergence of New Spiritual Paths*. Princeton, NJ: Princeton University Press.

—Unpublished. "Studying Religion\s as Worldviews and Ways of Life." Gunning Lectures on Worldviews and Ways of Life, University of Edinburgh, March 2018.

Taves, Ann, and Egil Asprem. 2017. "Experience as Event: Event Cognition and the Study of (Religious) Experience." *Religion, Brain & Behavior* 7: 43–62.

Taves, Ann, Egil Asprem, and Elliot Ihm. 2018. "Psychology, Meaning Making, and the Study of Worldviews: Beyond Religion and Non-Religion." *Psychology of Religion and Spirituality* 10(3): 207–17.

Taves, Ann, and Steven C. Harper. 2016. "Joseph Smith's First Vision: New Methods for the Study of Experience-Related Texts." *Mormon Studies Review* 3: 53–84.

Index

A Course in Miracles (ACIM), 17–18
Ancient religions, 39, 46–52, 119
Appraisal processes, 7–8, 11, 13–14, 16–17, 57, 78, 82, 115, 122
Astral projection, 15–16
Attribution, 6–7, 13, 57, 60, 72, 76–78, 118, 121–22
Autism, 3, 72–80, 121–22

Basic concepts (BC), 5–6, 9, 18, 32, 35, 37

CI scheme and measure, 62–63
Complex cultural concepts (CCC), 3, 5–9, 15–16, 18, 22, 31–32, 35, 37, 48, 71, 78, 81, 94, 104, 107, 116
Computer-aided text analysis, 85
Consilience, 5–6, 10–11, 26–27, 32, 35–36, 39, 41, 44, 46, 82–83, 94, 101, 107–109, 121
Counterintuitiveness, 43, 55–56, 58, 61–66, 115–17
Cultural transmission, 61–62, 108

Darshan, 66
Deference, 93
Dreaming as primary source of religion, 55, 58

Embodied experience, 9, 32, 72, 75–79. 121
Emotions and narrative, 44–47
Erudition mode, 34
Esotericism, 7–8, 18, 28, 77, 104
Events and event cognition, 10–11, 13–15, 17–18, 116–18

Fantasy, fantastic narrative, 3, 39, 42–44, 47, 74–77
Fractionated-approach, 3, 55–56, 115

Generational, 3, 72, 76–78

Identity, 44–47, 50, 105, 107
Imaginary, 22, 74–75, 61, 116
Institutions and Institutionalization, 8, 55, 57, 62, 66, 75, 84, 102, 109, 122
Interdisciplinary, 3, 11, 71–73, 79

K-means clustering, 91

Martin, Luther H., 27–28, 32–33, 35, 114–15
McCutcheon, Russell T., 27, 29–30, 35
MCI theory (minimal counterintuitiveness), 61–62, 116
Media, 3, 40–42, 76–77, 79, 118–19
Millenials, 72, 78
Moral Foundations Dictionary, 85–86
Moral foundations theory, 3, 84–85, 121
Moral models, 28
Mormonism, 17–18

Narrative, narrativity, 14–15, 17, 40–47, 51, 57, 63–64, 73–76, 79, 82, 117–18, 121
Nepal, 63, 115
Neurocognition, 8, 18, 56, 59–60
New mechanical philosophy, 9, 12, 32, 34
New mechanism, 8–9, 11–12, 103–104, 120–23
Nightmare, 59–60

Objectification of Islam, 94
Objective models, 115
Occulture, 72, 77–79, 121

Piecemeal-approach, 55, 66
Popper, Karl, 34
Popular culture, 3, 39, 40, 47, 50, 52, 72, 74, 77, 119–20
Predictive coding-approach, 1, 60, 77, 106
Predictive processing, 3, 20–21, 101, 105–107

Reduced sense of agency during dreaming, 60
Religious experience, 2–3, 6–7, 13–15, 39, 44, 61, 82
REM/NREM sleep, 59–60
Reverse engineering, 3, 6, 7, 9, 31, 37, 101, 103–105, 107–108

Sacredness, 57
Salafism, 92–93
Science mode, 34–35

Sense-making, 77–79, 121–22
Shiva, 65–66
Simplicity rule, 62, 65
Social frames, 40–41, 43, 46
Social Mapping, 56
Specialness, 57–58, 62, 66
Supernatural agency, 75–76, 79, 105
Supernatural experience, 75, 121

Threat Simulation (theory), 56
Vishnu, 64, 66

Wiebe, Donald, 27–28, 32–33, 35, 114–15
Worldviews, 1, 10, 14, 18–22, 39, 47, 49–51, 73, 103, 105, 108–109, 117, 119, 123

www.ingramcontent.com/pod-product-compliance
Lightning Source LLC
Chambersburg PA
CBHW061958220426
43662CB00011B/1734